The
POWER
of
KINDNESS

ALSO BY PIERO FERRUCCI

What We May Be

Inevitable Grace

What Our Children Teach Us

The Child of Your Dreams
(with Laura Huxley)

Jeremy P. Tarcher/Penguin

a member of Penguin Group (USA) Inc.

New York

The

POWER

of

KINDNESS

The Unexpected Benefits of
Leading a Compassionate Life

PIERO FERRUCCI

Translated by Vivien Reid Ferrucci

JEREMY P. TARCHER/PENGUIN
Published by the Penguin Group
Penguin Group (USA) Inc., 375 Hudson Street, New York, New York 10014, USA •
Penguin Group (Canada), 90 Eglinton Avenue East, Suite 700, Toronto, Ontario
M4P 2Y3, Canada (a division of Pearson Penguin Canada Inc.) • Penguin Books Ltd,
80 Strand, London WC2R 0RL, England • Penguin Ireland, 25 St Stephen's Green, Dublin 2,
Ireland (a division of Penguin Books Ltd) • Penguin Group (Australia),
250 Camberwell Road, Camberwell, Victoria 3124, Australia (a division of Pearson Australia
Group Pty Ltd) • Penguin Books India Pvt Ltd, 11 Community Centre, Panchsheel Park,
New Delhi–110 017, India • Penguin Group (NZ),
Cnr Airborne and Rosedale Roads, Albany, Auckland 1310, New Zealand
(a divison of Pearson New Zealand Ltd) • Penguin Books (South Africa) (Pty) Ltd,
24 Sturdee Avenue, Rosebank, Johannesburg 2196, South Africa

Penguin Books Ltd, Registered Offices: 80 Strand, London WC2R 0RL, England

Most Tarcher/Penguin books are available at special quantity discounts for bulk purchase
for sales promotions, premiums, fund-raising, and educational needs. Special books or book
excerpts also can be created to fit specific needs. For details, write Penguin Group (USA) Inc.
Special Markets, 375 Hudson Street, New York, NY 10014.

Library of Congress Cataloging-in-Publication Data

Ferrucci, Piero.
[Forza della gentilezza. English]
The power of kindness : the unexpected benefits of leading a compassionate life /
Piero Ferrucci ; translated to English by Vivien Reid Ferrucci.
p.   cm.
Includes bibliographical references.
ISBN 1-58542-519-2
1. Kindness.   2. Conduct of life.   I. Title.
BJ1533.K5F4713   2006   2006043865
177'.7—dc22

Printed in the United States of America
3   5   7   9   10   8   6   4   2

Book design by Meighan Cavanaugh

CONTENTS

PREFACE

This is a book after my own heart. Piero Ferrucci has drawn on both his broad experience as a psychotherapist and what I think of as fundamental human values to write on the importance of kindness. What I particularly appreciate about his presentation is that he makes kindness the starting point, the fount from which flow so many other positive qualities, such as honesty, forgiveness, patience, and generosity. It is a compelling and encouraging approach.

I believe that if we stop to think, it is clear that our very survival, even today, depends upon the acts and kindness of so many people. Right from the moment of our birth, we are under the care and kindness of our parents; later in life, when facing the sufferings of disease and old age, we are again dependent on the kindness of others. If at the beginning and end of our lives we depend upon others' kindness, why then in the middle, when we have the opportunity, should we not act kindly toward others?

Kindness and compassion are among the principal things that make our lives meaningful. They are a source of lasting happiness and joy. They are the foundation of a good heart, the heart of one who acts out of a desire to help others. Through kindness, and thus through affection, honesty, truth, and justice toward everyone else, we ensure our own benefit. This is a matter of common sense. Consideration for others is worthwhile because our happiness is inextricably bound up with the happiness of others. Similarly, if society suffers, we ourselves suffer. On the other hand, the more our hearts and minds are afflicted with ill will, the more miserable we become. Therefore, we cannot avoid the necessity of kindness and compassion.

On a simple, practical level, kindness creates a sense of warmth and openness that allows us to communicate much more easily with other people. We discover that all human beings are just like us, so we are able to relate to them more easily. That generates a spirit of friendship in which there is less need to hide what we feel or what we are doing. As a result, feelings of fear, self-doubt, and insecurity are automatically dispelled, while at the same time other people find it easier to trust us, too. What is more, there is increasing evidence that cultivating positive mental states like kindness and compassion definitely leads to better psychological health and happiness.

It is tremendously important that we try to make something positive of our lives. We were not born for the purpose of causing trouble and harming others. For our life to be of value, as Piero Ferrucci amply demonstrates here—and I am grateful to him for expressing it so clearly—we need to foster and nurture such basic good human qualities as warmth, kindness, and compassion. If we can do that, our lives will become meaningful, happier and more peaceful; we will make a positive contribution to the world around us.

—His Holiness the Dalai Lama
May 2004

INTRODUCTION

The little old lady no longer bothered to eat. Alone in the world, she felt forgotten by everyone. She was so depressed, she could not even swallow. The very idea of ingesting food was too much for her. Closed in her silent sadness, she was simply waiting for death.

At this point, Millina enters the scene. Millina was my aunt. Every afternoon she would do her rounds, taking care of homeless people, the elderly forgotten in nursing homes, neglected children, the outcasts and the maladjusted, the dying. She would try to make them feel a little better.

Millina meets the lady who no longer eats. She talks to her and gets her to talk a little too. In a faint voice, the old lady tells Millina about her sons and daughters, how they are too busy to look after her. No one comes to visit anymore. She has no illness. She is merely exhausted because she cannot manage to eat, and she cannot manage to eat because she is too exhausted.

"How would you like some ice cream?" Millina asks. It's a strange idea, giving ice cream to a dying person. But it works. With every spoonful, ever so slowly, some color, voice, and life return to the old lady.

It's simple, it's ingenious: Give a tasty, easily ingested food to someone who finds it hard to eat, and it will give her a quick lift. But this explanation is only part of the picture. The ice cream solution came to Millina only because she had taken the woman to heart. Because she had seen that this lady needed not only food, but above all care and attention—just what all of us need, as we need oxygen. Before the ice cream, it was the warmth of solidarity that the lady received, and what brought color back to her face was not merely food but, more significantly, a simple act of kindness.

Kindness? It may strike us as absurd to even approach the subject: Our world is full of violence, war, terrorism, devastation. And yet life goes on precisely because we are kind to one another. No newspaper tomorrow will tell of a mother who read a bedtime story to her child, or a father who prepared breakfast for his children, of someone who listened with attention, of a friend who cheered us up, of a stranger who helped us carry a suitcase. Many of us are kind without even knowing it. We do what we do simply because it is right.

My neighbor Nicola is always busy, yet he will never miss an opportunity to be of help. Whenever my wife, my children, and I have to go to the airport from our home in the country, he offers to take us. Afterward, he drives our car back home, puts it in the garage, and takes out the battery if we are away for long. Then he comes to fetch us at the airport when we return—in freezing cold or oppressive heat, he will be there.

Why does he do it? What makes him give up half a day, at any hour, to do us a favor when he could choose other more urgent or pleasant tasks? He could simply drop us at the nearest train station. But no, it is door-to-door service. He always finds a way to give his support wherever he can.

This is pure, disinterested kindness. However special it may sound, it is by no means exceptional. On the contrary, it comprises a great deal of human interactions. We hear about robberies and murders, but the world goes on thanks to people like Nicola. The fabric of our life is made of care, solidarity, mutual service. These qualities are so embedded in our daily events that we may not even notice them.

To receive kindness does us good. Think of a time someone has been kind to you, in a big or a small way: A passerby gave you directions to reach the station or a stranger threw herself in a river to save you from drowning. What effect did it have on you? Probably a beneficial one, because if someone helps us when we need it, we feel relief. And everyone likes to be heard, treated with warmth and friendliness, understood, and nourished.

Something similar happens on the other side of the equation: Giving kindness does us as much good as receiving it. If you accept the broad definition of kindness that I will outline in this book, you can safely say—and scientific research confirms it—that kind people are healthier and live longer, are more popular and productive, have greater success in business, and are happier than others. In other words, they are destined to live a much more interesting and fulfilling life than those who lack this quality. They are much better equipped to face life in all its savage unpredictability and frightening precariousness.

But I can already hear an objection: Suppose we are kind in order to feel better and live longer. Wouldn't we be perverting the very nature of kindness? We would make it calculated and self-interested, and therefore it would no longer be kindness. How true! Kindness derives its purpose from itself, not from other motives. The true benefit of kindness is being kind. Perhaps more than any other factor, kindness gives meaning and value to our life, raises us above our troubles and our battles, and makes us feel good about ourselves.

In a certain sense, all the scientific studies showing the advantages of kindness are useless—useless as incentives because the sole incentive to kindness can be none other than the desire to help, the pleasure of being generous and attentive to other people's lives. These studies, however, have extraordinary importance from another point of view: They help us understand who we are. If we are healthier when we are caring, empathic, and open to others, it means we are born to be kind. If we push our way forward, cultivate hostile thoughts, or bear lifelong grudges, we will not be at our best. And if we ignore or repress our positive qualities, we may harm ourselves and others. As psychiatrist Alberto Alberti maintains, love that is not expressed becomes hate, joy that is not enjoyed becomes depression. Yes, we are *designed* to be kind.

Research is a useful tool for understanding ourselves, but not the only and definitive one. The wisdom of the ages, great art, and our own intuition can help us here. As we shall see, kindness in all its aspects can become an extraordinary inner adventure that radically changes our way of thinking and being, and moves us briskly along in our personal and spiritual growth. Several spiritual traditions see kindness and altruism as the key to salvation or liberation. For instance, here is how the Buddha lists the benefits of kindness. Sharon Salzberg quotes him in her beautiful book *Lovingkindness*. If you are kind:

1. You will sleep easily.
2. You will wake easily.
3. You will have pleasant dreams.
4. People will love you.
5. Devas (celestial beings) and animals will love you.
6. Devas will protect you.
7. External Dangers (poisons, weapons and fire) will not harm you.
8. Your face will be radiant.
9. Your mind will be serene.

10. You will die unconfused.
11. You will be reborn in happy realms.

Great poets have also seen, in love and the sense of unity with all living beings, the essence of our lives and our greatest victory. Dante, in *The Divine Comedy,* for example, after going through hell and purgatory, and after seeing human perversion and unhappiness in all of its forms, rises to heaven, and toward the end of his journey, at the center of the mystical rose, he sees a "laughing beauty"—it is the Madonna, the archetype of femininity. According to some interpreters, the whole of *The Divine Comedy* is a voyage of self-discovery and a man's reunion with his feminine part, his lost soul, where soul implies the heart and the capacity to feel and love.

Goethe, in his *Faust,* the masterpiece on which he worked all his life, arrives by a different route to the same conclusion. According to the pact with the devil, Faust must find a moment in his life that makes his existence worthwhile—otherwise he will be forever captive of the Evil One. He looks for happiness in the ecstasy of pleasure, the euphoria of power and wealth, and the grandiose dream of scientific knowledge. But he does not find it there. In the end, when all seems to be lost and the Devil moves arrogantly forward to claim his victory, he finds fulfillment in the eternal feminine—love and tenderness and warmth.

Let us return to earth. It should be clear by now that I am speaking of true kindness. Heaven save us from the fakes—self-interested politeness, calculated generosity, superficial etiquette. And also from kindness against one's will. What's more embarassing than someone doing us a favor out of a sense of guilt? Psychoanalysts speak of yet another type of kindness—one that hides anger, a "reaction formation." The idea of being full of rage upsets us, so we unconsciously repress this dark side and act in a kind way. But this is false and contrived, and has nothing to do with what, in our heart, we really care for. Finally, weakness masquerades sometimes as kindness: You say yes when you mean no, you go along because you want to be nice, you acquiesce because you are afraid. A person who is too good and submissive ends up a loser.

So let us have none of this. My thesis is that true kindness is a strong, genuine, warm way of being. It is the result of the interplay among several qualities, such as warmth, trust, patience, loyalty, gratitude, and many others. Each chapter in this book will be about kindness seen from the standpoint of one of these qualities. It will be a variation on the same musical theme.

Without even one of these qualities, kindness is less convincing and less true. Each of these qualities alone is sufficient, if we evoke and cultivate it, to revolutionize our psyche and change our life radically. Together, their action is even more effective and profound. From this perspective, kindness is synonymous with mental health.

The gifts of kindness and its qualities are various. Why are grateful people more efficient? Why are those who feel a sense of belonging less depressed? Why do altruistic people enjoy better health, and trusting individuals live longer? Why is it that if you smile, you are perceived as more attractive? Why is it advantageous to take care of a pet? Why do those elderly who can talk more with others have less probability of contracting Alzheimer's disease? And why do children who receive more love and attention grow healthier and more intelligent? Because all these attitudes and behaviors, which are all aspects of kindness, bring us closer to what we are meant to do and to be. It is so elementary: If we relate better with others, we feel better.

Kindness, as we will see, has many facets. But its essence is as simple as can be. We will find that kindness is a way of making *less* effort. It is the most economic attitude there is, because it saves us much energy that we might otherwise waste in suspicion, worry, resentment, manipulation, or unnecessary defense. It is an attitude that, by eliminating the inessential, brings us back to the simplicity of being.

Kindness has to do with what is tenderest and most intimate in us. It is an aspect of our nature that we often do not express fully—especially men in our culture, but also women—because we are afraid that if this vulnerable side comes to light, we might suffer, be offended, ridiculed, or exploited. We will find rather, that we suffer by not expressing it. And that by touching this nucleus of tenderness, we enliven our entire affective world, and we open ourselves to countless possibilities of change.

This task is not always easy. The culture we live in will often sabotage us. That is because we all are in the midst of a "global cooling." Human relations are becoming colder. Communications are becoming more hurried and impersonal. Values such as profit and efficiency are taking on greater importance at the expense of human warmth and genuine presence. Family affections and friendships suffer and are less lasting. Signs of this decline are everywhere, visible especially when they touch us in the small catastrophes of everyday life.

You make a phone call to talk with a person and you hear a digital voice presenting a list of options. You park your car and find out the parking attendant has been replaced by a meter. You wait for a letter from a friend and receive an e-mail. The farm you loved is gone, and in its place stands a cement building. You notice that older people are not as well cared for and respected as they used to be. Your doctor concentrates on the test results instead of listening to you and looking at you. And rather than playing ball in the backyard, kids move in the virtual world of video games. At the same time, human warmth, subtracted from everyday life, is now *sold* as a product: "homemade ice cream," bread baked "the way it used to be," pasta just like Grandma used to make, the car that makes you feel you are back in the womb, the phone that allows you to be in touch.

Human feelings do not always remain the same. They change in emphasis and tone through the centuries. Thus we can talk about a history of emotions. I am convinced that we are going through an Ice Age of the heart, which began more or less with the Industrial Revolution and continues in our post-industrial age. The causes of this Ice Age are many: new living conditions and forms of work, the establishing of new technologies, the decline of the extended family, the great migrations in which people are uprooted from their birthplace, the weakening of values, the fragmentation and superficiality of the contemporary world, the accelerating pace of life.

Do not misunderstand me—I am not pining for the good old days. On the contrary, I think we are living in an extraordinary epoch. If we wish to cultivate solidarity, kindness, care for others, we have more knowledge, instruments, and possibilities than ever before. Still, the Ice Age we are passing through is worrisome, and I am not surprised that it goes hand in hand with the epidemic of depression and panic attacks, probably the two psychological disturbances most linked to lack of warmth and of a reassuring and protective community, and to a weakened sense of belonging.

Kindness itself might seem lightweight, and yet it is a central factor in our lives. It has surprising power to transform us, perhaps more than any other attitude or technique. The great English writer Aldous Huxley was a pioneer in the study of philosophies and techniques aimed at developing human potential, including such diverse approaches as Vedanta, psychedelics, bodywork, meditation, hypnotic trance, and Zen. Toward the end of his life, he said, in a lecture, "People often ask me what is the most effective technique for transforming their life. It is a little embarassing that after years and years of research and experimentation, I have to say that the best answer is—just be a little kinder."

This is also the Dalai Lama's philosophy. His motto, "My religion is kindness," is one of the simplest, most efficacious statements I have ever heard. It is like an $E = mc^2$ of the Spirit—a universal principle that contains an enormous potential for good, and cuts through all dogma, inviting us to concentrate on an essential theme and showing us the simplest way to liberation.

But wait. While no doubt we are altruistic, we are at the same time the cruelest species on the planet. Our history is full of wickedness and horrors. Yet a unilateral and fixed view of human nature is both false and dangerous. The image of primitive humans fighting for survival through violence and bullying is misleading. If our long evolution has been successful, it is also because we have been kind. We nurture and protect our young for much longer than all other mammals. The solidarity of humans has facilitated communication and cooperation. That is how we have faced adversity, developed our intelligence and our multiple resources. It is thanks to the warmth and care we have given and received that, so far, we have been winning—because we have helped one another. Now, in the twenty-first century, a kind individual is no bizarre mutant in a violent world. He or she is a human who knows how best to use those faculties that have helped us in the course of our evolution.

No doubt about it, we would all be much better off in a kinder world. Kindness, in its broadest sense, is the universal remedy— first, for the individual, for we can be well only if we are able to care for ourselves, to love ourselves. And then for all of us, because if we have better relationships, we feel and do better.

Kindness is essential at all levels of education since we learn more in an atmosphere of warmth and attention than of indifference and repression. A child treated with tenderness grows healthily, a student who receives respect and attention can make much progress. In health, too, kindness is a necessary ingredient: Patients who are treated with empathy and care suffer less and heal sooner.

And what about business and commerce? Here again we reach the same conclusion. Firms that exploit their workers, degrade the environment, deceive the consumer, and create a waste culture, will perhaps gain in the short term, but in the long run they compete less favorably than those that, in their own interests, do not take advantage of employees, respect the environment, and place themselves at the service of clients.

In the political arena, kindness is the giving up of domination and vendetta, and the recognition of others' points of view, their needs, and their history. Violence and war, on the other hand, appear more and more as remarkably gross and inefficient ways for resolving the world's problems—a method that generates rage and thus new violence, chaos, waste of resources, suffering, and poverty.

Finally, kindness is urgent in our relationship with our living environment. If we do not respect and love nature, do not treat her with loving kindness and the awe that she deserves, we will end up intoxicated by our own poisons.

We still do not know, however, who we really are. The definitive version does not yet exist. We are capable of the most horrendous crimes and the most sublime acts. Neither of these two potentials is established enough to allow us to define it as a dominant trait of human nature.

It is up to us. It is a choice in the life of each of us—to take the road of selfishness and abuse, or the way of solidarity and kindness. In this exciting but dangerous moment of human history, kindness is not a luxury, it is a necessity. Maybe if we treat each other, and our planet, a little better, we can survive, even thrive. And by becoming kinder, we might end up discovering that we have given ourselves the best, the most intelligently selfish gift.

HONESTY

Everything Becomes Easier

Albert Schweitzer was invited by the Norwegian royalty to a banquet in his honor after he had won the Nobel Prize for Peace. A plate of herring was placed before him—a food he could not stomach. He did not want to appear impolite by refusing it, so when the queen turned away for a moment, he quickly put the herring in the pocket of his jacket. "You certainly ate the herring fast," commented the queen with a funny smile. "Would you like some more?"

Schweitzer had not wished to offend and had solved the problem by hiding the dinner in his pocket. He too was unable to say no—at least on that occasion. Perhaps, despite his innocent trick, he had not completely digested the meal, for years later he felt impelled to tell the story. It makes me wonder how many of us are walking around with herring in our pockets.

Honesty is often embarrassing. The truth can be sharp and uncomfortable, the truth-teller tactless, the receiver disturbed by the revelation: "I don't like the way they have cut your hair," "Your dinner is bland," "I don't feel like being with you tonight," "You need deodorant," "Mom, I'm gay." How does all this fit in with kindness, which is by definition supposed to be comfortable, warm, and soft as feather down? Can honesty and kindness coexist? Or do we have to choose?

A while ago, my family and I boarded a train without having bought tickets. We were going to buy them from the conductor on the train. When he approached us, I said, "We arrived at the station at the last moment, so we would like to pay now."

"No, that's not how it went," my wife, Vivien, surprisingly piped up. "We had plenty of time." The conductor looked perplexed. Vivien didn't want to get me in trouble, she is simply incapable of telling a lie. Yet I was also telling the truth. We had arrived at the station ten minutes before departure, hardly sufficient time for me to familiarize myself with an unfriendly ticket machine.

The conductor accepted my explanation and cast me a look of clandestine solidarity. I thought that maybe he was married, too.

This reluctance to lie, however embarrassing it may be at times, is an aspect of human nature—a spontaneous reaction. Some time earlier, my wife had been shopping with our 6-year-old son, Jonathan. She was returning a T-shirt, exchanging it for a different size, when Jonathan, full of goodwill, exclaimed: "But Mommy, we didn't get that shirt here! You bought it at another store." After a moment of embarrassment, the mystery was clarified: That other shop was part of the same chain of stores, and the exchange, although somewhat unusual, was permitted. Children's candor is all very well, unless it interferes with our everyday compromises.

At first it seems that telling the truth is more uncomfortable and difficult than telling a lie. And it is just this conviction that leads us to lie in order to hide our weaknesses and avoid giving explanations or getting into trouble—out of laziness or perhaps out of fear. Yet it is falsehood that in the long run is more difficult and complicates our life.

The lie-detector machine is based on this very principle. When we lie, we subject our body to a stress. The stress is measurable: sweating, heart rate, muscle tension, and blood pressure increase. This ordeal is invisible to us but easily revealed by scientific instruments. When we lie, we are clutching at straws. If we pretend, we are making a big effort, because we must invent a lie and feel anxious in case we are found out. We try to avoid being unmasked, and thus perpetuate our anxiety.

What a job! Computerized scanning of cerebral activity shows that when we lie, our brain has to carry out a series of complex operations that are needless when we tell the truth. The scientist who invented this method maintains that the brain tells the truth "by default"—meaning that we are programmed to be sincere.

To be transparent is a relief. Muddy water hides a host of unpleasant surprises. Clear water shows us the bottom of the sea—the rubbish and debris if they are there, but also the multicolored fish, shells, starfish. Honesty allows us to look into someone's eyes and through them into the heart, because there is no veil, no fiction. It allows us to let ourselves be seen—and look back without averting our eyes.

Honesty exists in both directions—in our interactions with ourselves and with others. To know yourself, said the psychologist Sydney Jourard in his book *The Transparent Self,* is the sine qua non of mental health. But we can hardly know ourselves in isolation: We must first let ourselves be known by someone else, without bluffing or hiding. For Jourard, all neurotic symptoms, such as fear of leaving the house or depression, are nothing more than screens we erect in order to hide ourselves from others. As soon as we become more transparent, we start to feel better. However, we can also, on a parallel course, learn to be honest with ourselves, to look with unflinching eyes into our inner world and not turn away. As Polonius says in *Hamlet,* "This above all: to thine own self be true, and it must follow, as the night the day, thou canst not then be false to any man."

Consider an extreme case: eccentrics. They are people who are honest with themselves, who have not the slightest intention of pretending to be other than what they are, and who profoundly honor what they feel. For this reason, they engage in practices that may seem to us strange and unconventional. A study, some years old now, found that eccentrics were longer-lived and happier than average. The author of the study wrote an interesting book about them. In it, you read about the man who always walked backward (thus he journeyed from California to Istanbul); the woman who collected what other people threw out, and bought an abandoned theater to house what she had accumulated; the man who rode around on a contraption that was half rocking-horse and half bicycle; the woman who every evening invited a group of rats to dinner; and so forth. Because eccentrics are not subject to the stress of having to conform to others' expectations, their immune system is stronger. They are healthier and happier.

These *are* extreme cases. Yet the theme is the same—honesty. We can all learn from eccentrics. In *The Divine Comedy,* Dante pictures the hypocrites in hell. They must go about with a heavy metal cape, gold on the outside, lead on the inside. It is infinitely exhausting toil to wear this shiny but false and weighty garb, which represents what they are not and never will be. Not having to pretend simplifies our life. On the other hand, pretending day after day to be someone you are not, requires enormous effort.

Let us return to the original question: Are honesty and kindness incompatible? Honesty, at times so tough, has a lot in common with kindness, though they might seem to be opposites. If kindness has falseness at its base, it is no longer kindness. It is a labored courtesy. It does not come from the heart, but from a fear of sticking one's neck out, of provoking strong reactions, or of facing accusation and argument. What do you prefer—genuine kindness, ready to tell the uncomfortable truth? Or the politeness of someone who avoids confrontation, declares himself to be having fun when he is bored, says yes when he means no, and smiles when in agony?

In my psychotherapy work, I have seen scores of people who have said yes when they really wanted to say no. They have said yes even to big commitments, such as marriage, the purchase of a house, a work contract. And they have let others make free use of their time and space. ("Why don't you come out with us this evening?" "Can you do this job for me?" "Will you look after my two cats while I'm away?" "Can I stay with you for a few weeks?" "Why of course.") The inability to utter the magic word has at times even led to catastrophe. It has made people live with someone they did not love, in a home they did not like, made them work at a job they hated, deprived them of their peace of mind. It has forced them to live a life that was not theirs, because they did not have the courage and honesty to say a simple, honest, firm word that would have saved their own life and the life of others: "*No.*"

In a famous children's book, *George and Martha,* two hippos of indeterminate age are the best of friends and go through the usual ups and downs of friendships. My favorite episode is when George visits Martha, who proudly prepares her specialty for dinner: split pea soup. George hates this dish, but does not have the heart to tell Martha. So while Martha is in the kitchen, he secretly pours the soup into his shoes, pretending to have eaten and enjoyed it. But Martha finds him out. After a few moments of embarrassment, the two of them agree that it is just because they are friends that they can tell each other the truth. Not having to eat a dish we do not like is a symbolic example. If we were to eat it, it would remain undigested, like anything we do unwillingly because we do not have the strength to refuse. Sometimes, in order to be kind, we first have to learn to look after ourselves.

TO ACT HONESTLY—EVEN AT THE RISK OF SAYING THE UN-pleasant truth, or of saying no and causing distress to others—if done with intelligence and tact, is the kindest thing to do, because it respects our own integrity and acknowledges in others the capacity to be competent and mature. A music teacher I know once said to me, "I feel I am kinder if I tell a student he has no talent, and advise him to stop his studies and find an interest to which he is better suited, rather than encourage him to continue. If, in order not to hurt him, I say something I do not believe, I deceive him, and perhaps prolong for years his hardship and defeat. If instead I say the truth, he might be unhappy at first, but at least he knows where he stands and can work out more clearly his next move. That to me is true kindness."

Just think how you felt if you ever discovered that someone was trying to protect you—by hiding the gravity of an illness, for example, or not telling you an unpleasant matter that was apparent to everyone, or simply not letting you know your makeup was a mess, or your fly was undone. All out of politeness, to protect you. The result is a feeling of being underestimated or even betrayed: "Why didn't someone tell me?"

But honesty is a conquest. We have to learn it gradually, and in this way become stronger and more mature. The ancient Aztecs believed we are born without a face and that we must win our faces bit by bit as we grow. We can do this only by honoring truth. If we lie, or if we are not clear about what we want to say, we will have a face without form. Only with an authentic face will we be able to come out of Tlalticpac, the world of dreams.

TO BE HONEST ALSO MEANS TO RECOGNIZE A PROBLEM rather than to pretend there is none. Some time ago, my son Emilio was going back to school after vacation. He did not like the idea at all and was filled with anxiety. To him, the approach of school days was like a monster that threatened him and wanted to squash him. What is a parent supposed to do? I tried to lift his spirits, to distract him, convince him it was not as bad as it seemed, but in vain. Then I hit upon the idea of offering him something I thought would do the trick. I offered Emilio something that is almost taboo in our family: French fries at a fast-food place. Usually anything that is prohibited appeals to Emilio, especially junk food. I thought I had the ace up my sleeve. But no. Emilio's reply ought to be chiseled in stone: "Dad, you don't solve problems with French fries."

Touché. You don't pretend problems do not exist, and you can't solve them with ephemeral distractions. You have to face them with open-eyed honesty. Offering French fries to my son in order to console and distract him from his anxiety was by no means a kind act. I was simply choosing the easier option—far too easy. I had found a comfortable way out. His response was a lesson in honesty.

But honesty does not concern only the difficult, unpleasant aspects in life. Even more it concerns the creative and beautiful ones. Because often, strange as it might seem, we hide those very aspects: our tenderness, goodwill, original thoughts, our capacity for being moved. We do this partly out of a sense of reserve: We don't want to overwhelm others with our gushing emotions. But mostly we do it to protect ourselves. We don't want others to see us like that. We would feel weak, exposed, perhaps ridiculous. Better to appear a bit cynical, even hard, or, at the very least, not so dangerously open. In that way, however, we separate from the most spiritual and beautiful part of ourselves—and prevent others from seeing it.

And that is not all. Lying has a thousand faces, the truth only one. We can pretend to have many emotions we don't really have, to be many people we are not. But if we stop pretending, all the artifices and the efforts to hold our life together fall away. What a relief.

When I was in the military, there was a fellow serviceman who liked to play the braggart. He often boasted about having won the world championship in swearing (I later found out it had been a village competition). He was the kind who always outdid you, whatever you said. One evening he and I were talking of this and that, when suddenly his face changed. He started to speak about his fear of death, about the void, about love. He became a completely different person, far more profound and true. It was much more worthwhile spending time with him like that. I told him so, and asked him why he had decided to take off his mask that evening. He answered, "Sometimes you have to let go, and just speak the truth."

Like all of us, at times I have conveyed emotional misinformation. I can understand people who do not want to show their true feelings; sometimes reserve is perfectly appropriate. But other times it is not. In my work as psychotherapist, I often hear both terrible and beautiful stories, and I am frequently moved. Is it right that my client notice this, or is it important that I hide behind an impassive mask? Opinions on this point abound. I do not think a psychotherapist should always disclose his emotions, because it could cause harm and create misunderstanding. Yet psychotherapy is only beneficial in a good relationship, and a relationship is good only if it is honest.

Once while listening to the story of a client, I was deeply moved. She noticed and told me so. I tried to hide my emotion, but she didn't believe it for a second. In that moment I realized how weak and awkward we are when we try to hide our feelings. And how important it is, within limits of tact and good taste, to be honest and freely show what we feel and who we are. So when are we kinder: when we hide our warmth, our dreams, our wonder, our humor, or when we reveal them?

Thus, not only is honesty compatible with genuine kindness, it is the very basis of kindness. False kindness pollutes. As long as you are not living in the truth, you cannot really communicate with others, you cannot have trust, you cannot relate. As long as you do not call the hard realities by name, you are living in the land of dreams. There is no room for you and me there, but only for harmful illusions. Inasmuch as we lie, we live a life devoid of reality. And kindness cannot exist in a world of masks and phantoms.

WARMTH

The Temperature of Happiness

Many years ago, my work took me to an American city on a winter's night. My flight had been delayed. I happened to be without cash, had not eaten, and it was cold. Also, there was a blackout in the part of town where I was supposed to stay, so I was also in the dark. Deprived of nearly every protection offered by civilization, I felt at the mercy of the irrational. Even though reason told me that I was not in any real danger, all my primitive alarm systems were switched on: hunger, dark, cold, no point of reference, no friendly presence. I had already reached the point of not knowing what to do. I was on the verge of panic.

Suddenly, as I was walking down the street, I heard my name called in the darkness. I have never been happier to hear it. And I have never been so deeply touched by a voice. It was the friend I was supposed to meet, and who—don't ask me how—had managed to find me in the dark. The rescuing voice was warmth itself.

In that moment, or rather, a little later, after I had eaten and was able to function normally again, I saw how precarious the human situation is—how defenseless and vulnerable we are in an imper-sonal and distracted world. I saw how the condition of babies, so much in need of care, affection, and warmth, is really the condition of all of us. Every day, countless people die or die a little bit for want of warmth: children left alone; underpaid and exploited workers; old people, lonely and forgotten by everyone in the anonymous world of big cities. And every day, thousands of people compensate for their chronic loveless state by all kinds of substitutes: filling themselves with food, pursuing loveless sex, seeking illusory happi-ness in the wonderlands of consumerism, or becoming violent.

Usually it is the sense of touch we associate most of all with warmth. But sound, which is a form of touch at a distance, can bring us warmth when we are out of reach. We just saw how, when I was lost in an unfamiliar place, I was rescued by a voice.

A woman I know, let's call her Dorothea, tells me another story. Every evening she hears her neighbors' baby girl crying in the apart-ment next to hers. The parents put the child to sleep alone in the dark. The baby cries for a long time while the parents watch televi-sion. The baby's desperate crying expresses all her anguish, her soli-tude. What should Dorothea do? She is uncertain. Speaking to the parents might make things worse. She decides to sing. Just as she can hear the baby, the baby can hear her. Every evening when they put the baby to bed, Dorothea sings her sweet lullabies, talks to her through the thin walls, consoles and comforts her. The baby hears the invisible friendly voice, stops crying, and falls peacefully asleep. The warmth of a stranger's voice has saved her from the icy cold of loneliness.

HOW DO YOU IMAGINE HELL? SMOKE, FIRE, GLOWING PITCH-forks, the smell of roasting meat? We have always been told it was a hot place. Even a rationalist like Voltaire, when on his deathbed and seeing that a curtain had fallen into the fireplace and caught fire, exclaimed, with a mixture of irony and dismay, "*Déjà les flammes*— Already the flames!"

But are we really sure? Dante's *Inferno* describes the lowest, most terrible point in hell as a silent, icy place. The traitors, stained with the most evil of sins, have their heads immersed in an eternally frozen swamp. These damned souls are incapable of emotion and think nothing of betraying family, country, friends. Hell is the total absence of all feeling. It is the negation of warmth, a dark, frightening place where you are alone and without love.

Afterward, Dante climbs the Mount of Purgatory—a long and arduous ascent that represents the work of purification and strengthening necessary for finding ourselves. At the apex of Purgatory, after not seeing her for a very long time, Dante finds his old love, Beatrice, here representing Truth. Beatrice is cold to him: she does not run to embrace him. She wants him to feel the full weight of his forgetfulness. She reproaches him: Why did you neglect me? It is at once the tantrum of a furious woman and the imperious cry of Truth to those who for too long have trodden the wrong path. Dante is frozen, like the snow on the Apennine mountains. But under the rays of the spring sun, this snow thaws. Dante thaws too, and weeps. Once again he feels the warmth of emotion. Afterward, he is "pure, and ready to climb to the stars."

For Dante, warmth is the potential for all emotion, and therefore makes life itself possible. Warmth for him is also the prerequisite for transformation. As usual, a poet understood what scientists and researchers discovered centuries later. We cannot live without the warmth and closeness of others. For decades, we have known that a baby cannot survive without a mother's warmth. Physical warmth— to be touched, cuddled, protected, nurtured, caressed, rocked—is not a luxury but a necessary condition for life. If babies do not get it, they die, and if they do not get enough of it, they do not thrive. As they grow up, they become fearful, neurotic, aggressive, and possibly criminal.

Like babies, we adults also need warmth—psychological warmth. Physical, too: sometimes we need to be touched and cuddled like babies. But mostly we need someone to talk to, someone who knows and appreciates us. Someone who cares about us. Warmth then becomes a metaphor. It is no longer just a biological necessity, it is a quality we see in someone's eyes, hear in her voice, sense in the way she greets us. It is at the very heart of kindness.

WARMTH HAS BECOME A COMMODITY: IF YOU TRULY WANT the divine, life-giving, pleasure-giving gift of warmth, and if you cannot find it in your own life, then I will sell it to you. On a huge orange billboard I have seen, is a gorgeous bowl of steaming vegetable soup, and underneath are the words, "That's *amore.*" It is a multinational frozen-foods ad. This is the situation: Everyone is too busy, so no one is welcoming you home this evening with hot and tasty vegetable soup. It is hard to imagine a more spot-on symbol of comforting, reassuring love. What solace, those spoonfuls, and what pleasure! And what relief to know that someone loves you and has prepared a bowl of sublime nourishment. But that someone is too busy now, or has perhaps forgotten you, or does not even exist. So here is a soup made by machine in a distant place and then frozen in a sterile packet. Don't worry, it defrosts straightaway. After all, it's the same thing, isn't it? Here it is, delicious, ready in minutes, and the same for everyone. Buy, eat, and keep quiet! Warmth is included in the price: "That's *amore.*"

It will be the same soup for everyone. But when there is real warmth, no one is the same as everyone else, just as no two soups are alike. We are all unique. We are all loved for who we are, with our qualities and with our faults. We are loved because we are irredeemably ourselves. But when warmth decreases, we are all the same—all anonymous. Just as warmth brings to light our personalities and makes us feel special and indispensable, coldness can turn us into nameless shadows.

I once had to go to the dermatologist. I did not see one doctor only, but a whole team of specialists. One of them, a woman, examined my foot for a long time with a lens, without saying anything. At the end of the consultation, when I was preparing to leave and after she had finished writing her notes, she raised her head and, seeing me there, gave a start: "Who are you? What are you doing here?" She had not realized that I was the owner of the foot. For her I was merely an image to be analyzed under a lens. She saw me then for the first time as a whole person. I made much more sense to her when I was just a foot without name or voice. That is anonymity.

Another aspect of warmth, which turns a biological reality into memory and metaphor, is closeness. Whoever is close is intimate and warm. Whoever is remote is inaccessible and cold. At the beginning of our lives, this is a physical fact. Whoever is close holds us and touches us, gives us warmth, is well known to us. A newborn baby knows its mother by her smell. Later, this closeness becomes more and more subjective. Someone close to us can also be thousands of miles away. Warmth becomes a more subtle but no less important quality. Intimacy is not only physical, but also psychological and spiritual. It is the capacity to enter and to let enter, to get to know and to allow to be known. To reveal our own dreams, our strangest and most embarrassing sides. To be without fear.

We often take warmth for granted and only notice it when it is gone. Then we understand its importance. This happened to me in regard to two funerals, many years apart. The first was that of my grandfather. I was riding, for the first time in my life, in the car carrying the coffin. From it I could see how the outside world was responding to our passage. It was a clearly visible reaction. People stopped and let us pass, some took their hats off, some made the sign of the cross. It signified respect and recognition: Someone had died and others were in mourning. I felt comforted: Death was no longer a lonely event.

Nearly thirty years later, my mother died. Same city, same itinerary and procedure. But times had changed. People passed, unaware and in a hurry. The town did not pause; everyone carried on with his own affairs. Not even a sign of recognition. I felt I was in a colder, more distracted world. Then I truly understood how important is warmth and the support of those around us.

However, there are many emotional obstacles to warmth and intimacy. We are afraid that if we come too close, or if we are too open, we will be invaded, controlled, or hurt. These are ancient fears, partly irrational, partly legitimate. We have taken millions of years to become individuals. It is natural for us to defend our victory. With too much intimacy, we are afraid that our borders will cease to exist, that we ourselves will be pulverized. But often these borders become barriers, the membranes ossify and no longer let anything through. We shut ourselves in the cold fortress of our solitude.

In one of Aesop's fables, the wind and the sun bet as to which one can get a wayfarer to undress first. The wind starts. It blows. But the traveler does not undress. It blows more strongly. The traveler remains dressed, in fact he pulls his cloak more tightly around him. The wind then blows as hard as it can. It blows a gale. A tornado. The traveler, far from undressing, clings to his clothes for dear life. Enter the sun. It does its job—it shines. Now there is no more wind.

It gets hot. The traveler takes his cloak off. The sun wins—not with strength but with warmth.

The benefits of warmth, if we include touching and talking, are enormous. Ashley Montagu, in his classic book, *Touching,* has demonstrated how touching boosts the health of all mammals—animals, children, adults. Another classic study, conducted in forty-nine cultures by neurophysiologist James W. Prescott, shows that in societies where physical affection is lavished on infants, invidious displays of wealth, incidence of theft, killling and torturing of enemies are all low. In societies where infant physical affection is low, instead slavery is present, the status of women is inferior, and the gods are depicted as aggressive. Prescott sees warmth during infancy, and openness to bodily pleasure, as the best and easiest way to transform our psychobiology of violence into one of peace.

In the last decades, various studies have confirmed what we have known instinctively for millennia. And in recent years, research has been even more specific. For children and adolescents, parents' warmth for their children helps them to feel good about themselves, to be independent, and to perform well at school. And what about adults? Ten thousand Israeli men were asked, among other questions about their health, habits, and circumstances, "Does your wife show you love?" A negative answer to this question was the best predictor for angina pectoris.

But even having someone to talk to, to fill the emptiness of solitude, is essential. For old people, the opportunity just to chat is useful in lowering the risk of Alzheimer's disease. Can this be a matter of mere intellectual stimulation? No. Another study shows that it is being touched that really helps old people who are afflicted with dementia to suffer less and be in a better mood.

. . .

IN THE 1950s, A GROUP OF HARVARD STUDENTS WAS SCREENED for a longitudinal research project. All the basic data about their lives were collected in detail. Thirty-six years later, 126 of the former students agreed to participate again in the research. They were divided in two groups; one consisting of those who described their parents as warm, patient, and affectionate; the other, of those who described them as impatient, cold, and brutal. The first group had a lower incidence than average of ulcers, alcoholism, and heart disease; the second group, a much higher than average. In the first group, 25 percent of the people had suffered from a major disease; in the second, 87 percent.

By now you will perhaps have noted a curious fact. While in this book we usually speak of benefits awaiting the *giver* of kindness, here we talking about benefits for the *receiver*. The contradiction is resolved if we ask ourselves: When we stroke a purring cat, who is giving and who is receiving warmth? Or, when we enjoy someone's company, who is warmed by the relationship? And when we hold a newborn baby, who gives and who receives the tenderness? If we give warmth, we do not end up feeling cold. The benefit is symmetrical. In giving our warmth—and so too our vital presence, our positive, nonjudgmental attitude, our heart—we can bring into the lives of those near to us vital, sometimes extraordinary, changes. And we, too, do not remain unchanged.

When a person has felt coldness and finds warmth, it is like discovering that life has infinitely more possibilities. Feelings are not an irritating variable but a great richness that allows us to know things we never even imagined. The heart has its reasons that reason knows not. Knowledge of the heart gives us the chance to know others, not as statistical data or lifeless puppets but as vibrant beings, full of hopes and dreams. Knowledge of the heart is instinctive, direct, wordless. You, as friend, know your friend needs you. You, partner, are aware that your partner is in difficulty, or that she is okay. You, parent, know how your child is feeling without having to ask.

Let us imagine a life in which all affection has disappeared, like a river that has dried up. Let us imagine that even the memory of warmth and affection has vanished. We move around each other without feeling. It is a world with precise and rigid borders, in which only numbers and hard facts count.

On the other hand, warmth can be overdone. We are all familiar with those intolerable individuals who want warmth at all costs, hug us and touch us and invade our privacy relentlessly. Sometimes coldness is necessary, and so is distance, and so are boundaries. Sometimes cold objectivity is not a bad thing. It may be refreshing to see the world around us without the screen of emotions and preferences.

But in the end, a world that is cold and lifeless is boring, if not altogether deadly. Let us imagine the opposite—our life pervaded with warmth and tenderness. We feel strong enough to be able to lower our defenses. We can bring relief and happiness by our mere presence, and we have clearer knowledge of the inner world of others, we have the capacity to see into the deeper thoughts and motivations of people. Love, friendship, kindness become the sense of our life and our highest value. Doesn't that feel right?

My son Jonathan told me that once on a school outing, tired after a long hike, he was lagging behind everybody and felt lonely and lost. But a kind friend waited for him and told him, "Come on, Jonathan, you can make it!" And he did make it. That was enough to help him. Jonathan calls it "a warming help": attention and a kind word in a difficult moment. It is perhaps what each of us needs, in our life's path, to make our next step forward.

FORGIVENESS

Live in the Present

Years ago, a friend of mine used to ask people, What is the most important thing in life? The answers fell within a predictable range—health, to love one another, financial security—and often came with an explanation, as if the person replying were not quite sure and wanted to justify the answer to herself as well. One day, my friend put the same question to her father. They were in the kitchen; he was making himself coffee. The answer was simple, calm and spontaneous. It needed no further comment: "To forgive."

My friend's father was Jewish, and his entire family had been exterminated in the Holocaust. (He later remarried and emigrated to Australia, where my friend was born.) I have seen the photos of his family. They are kept in an old tin box—all that remains of the family after the tragedy. They are photos of people like you and me, completely unaware of the impending doom.

The photo of a little girl struck me most of all. You look at it and can imagine her going to school, or playing, or talking with her parents. A beautiful little girl who exists no more. I have tried to understand how this man must have felt when he realized he had lost her—and with her, his wife, his mother and father, brother and sister, his work, his home. I have tried, but all I have managed, in a vague and blurred way, is to imagine the horror of that time, the incredulity, and then the unbearable pain.

And yet this man is capable of forgiving. Not only that, he can also single out forgiveness as *the* most important value in life. I regard his attitude as a magnificent victory. And it is thanks to this victory—more than to the miracles of electronics, genetics, or astronautics—that civilization is still possible. It is thanks to this man, and many others like him, that we have not plunged totally into barbarism.

Though maybe we have. Read the newspaper any day, and you will be struck by the amount of unresolved resentment on earth. To fully understand what this darkness entails for us all, I ask you to imagine a possibility, a paradox. Tomorrow morning we wake up and find that everyone has forgiven everything there was to forgive, and has found the courage to say sorry for any wrongs. Just think: What would happen if population X forgave population Y the terrible slaughter of many years ago? And what if ethnic group Z forgave ethnic group W, which in past centuries had oppressed it, violated its women, exploited its men, mistreated its children, and plundered its possessions? What if nations A and B acknowledged each other's right to exist freely, without fear and oppression, forgetting the wrongs both done and received? And what would happen if we woke up and discovered that even individuals had forgiven one another every injustice, and instead of recycling the past, could at last live fully in the present?

We would all breathe a sigh of relief. The atmosphere would be immeasurably happier and lighter. And many people would discover for the first time the wonder of living in the present moment

instead of constantly investing huge parts of themselves in recrimi-
nations and accusations, reliving events that are long past. Relations
between people would be open. And all the energy poured into
blame, hatred, prejudice, and revenge would instead circulate freely
and feed thousands of new projects.

Utopia, maybe. Forgiveness, however, is a definite possibility on a
smaller scale. But let us at once clear any misunderstandings: Because it is so precious and important, we must not mistake forgiveness for caricatures. First of all, it is not the same as condoning. If I
have been victim of an injustice in the past, I might be afraid that it
will be repeated or its gravity underestimated. I might fear that the
one who committed the injustice will get away with it, perhaps even
laugh behind my back. Therefore I might remain silent.

That is not it. Forgiveness means only that I do not want to continue feeding anger for an age-old wrong, hence ruin my life. I forgive, yes, but I keep well in mind the harm done to me, and I will be
mindful that it does not happen again. Someone who has forgiven
can still live in a world where injustice is not tolerated. He just does
not keep his alarm systems forever switched on, his guns always
aimed at the enemy.

Nor is forgiveness an act of self-righteousness, in which I affirm
my moral superiority and pat myself on the back for how noble and
generous I am, meanwhile thinking of the miserable fool who
wronged me, who is burning in hell for the mischief he has done.
No. Forgiveness is the inner act of making peace with the past and
of finally closing accounts.

This decision is not easy. On the contrary, it is, first of all, nonra-
tional, because accounts do not balance. How can you possibly forgive abuse that has gone on for years, such as a slander that has
ruined your life, or a betrayal that has disintegrated your family?
How can such damage be repaired? No words, no sum of money can

compensate, say, the loss of a loved one killed by a drunken driver. Forgiveness is contrary to all logic and mathematics. And forgiveness is also—or feels—dangerous: It exposes us not so much to repetition of the original harm as to feeling vulnerable and open. We feel vulnerable because our identity, like ivy that grows over an old column and clings to it, is attached to the wrong we have received. We feel that if we forgive, we lose our identity, and thus we feel insecure. Whereas if we do not forgive, the sense of outrage and indignation may offer some spurious strength, and support our whole personality. But do we really want that kind of support?

We do not even need to see forgiveness as the absence of resentment—an emotionally neutral void. Nor as the release of tension, like relaxing a muscle after tensing it for some time. Rather, forgiveness is a positive quality. It contains joy and faith in others, generosity of spirit. Illogical and surprising, sometimes sublime, it frees us from the ancient chains of resentment. Whoever forgives, feels uplifted.

In my work as a psychotherapist, when I suggest that possibility to a client ("Have you ever thought about forgiveness?"), I hesitate: Am I asking too much? Yet forgiveness is sometimes the only remedy for unspeakable suffering. I have seen many people who have forgiven. Some had suffered grave wrongs—odious bullying and injustices that had destroyed them, the ignominy of concentration camps, mistreatment as children, or sexual abuse. And yet they were able to forgive, and I have seen them in the very moment when they did so—extraordinary moments in which a nightmare ends and the forgivers feel reborn in joy.

I have also met many who have had great difficulty in forgiving even small wrongs. Their lives have become a permanent sullenness, a silent protest. The harm they have suffered appears before their eyes like an ever-repeating film. The muscles, breath, facial expression betray that they are still blocked in an offense done to them ten or twenty years before, and over which they are still recriminating, rising each day to live a life in response to that offense, as if they were still receiving it. Time does not exist in the unconscious: the past is a living present.

This unforgiving attitude brings ceaseless damage. We can compare an unforgiving person to a city whose traffic is completely congested. The roads are blocked; cars cannot move, and stand waiting with their exhausts running, the fumes poisoning the air. Garbage cannot be collected and lies rotting at the roadside in the overflowing bins. People are frustrated and immobilized, cannot work or communicate with others. No one enjoys life at all. Such is the state of nonforgiveness: stagnating rancor generating new rancor, and thus blocking vital energy, cramping thought, poisoning life.

We will better understand forgiveness if we remember a basic principle: Every element of a human being influences every other element. Emotions affect the body; the functioning of one organ affects all other organs; the past influences the present and the present the future; the relation with one person influences the relation with another; and so on. This multiplicity of interactions is especially noticeable with forgiveness. For instance, if twelve years ago my uncle Harry caused me woe and I have never forgiven him for it, the memory will influence my relationship with my cousin Joe, Harry's son. If I lent my car to my friend Shirley and she returned it with a bad scratch, the incident may change my attitude toward lending, or cars, or people. If I have had a wonderful and intense relationship with a woman but in the end was badly hurt, and if I have never forgiven that hurt, my relationship with the entire feminine world may be insecure, perhaps contaminated with mistrust and resentment.

And more still. It has been shown that our thoughts influence each cell in our body. Thought affects blood pressure and therefore the blood flow to every part of the body. The quality of our thoughts is felt throughout our organism. Will we make them thoughts of hatred and revenge, or of love and happiness?

In a famous experiment, subjects were asked to remember two experiences of betrayal, one in which they were betrayed by a parent, another by a partner. Meanwhile, they were hooked up to various stress-detector machines that checked their blood pressure, heart beat, muscle tension in the forehead, and galvanic skin response. The findings were revealing. It was immediately evident that the people fell into two distinct categories: high and low forgivers. Not only did the low forgivers show higher measurements of stress, the high forgivers had fewer health problems and had seen their doctors less frequently. In another study, it was shown that those who forgive, besides enjoying better physical health, suffer less from anxiety and depression. Forgiveness promotes physical and mental health.

In helping my clients to forgive, I have seen that two factors are useful. First, they must recognize the wrong they have felt, the sometimes terrible suffering that they might not yet have confronted. You cannot pretend nothing has happened. Before forgetting the injustice, you have to acknowledge and feel it fully. It is no good to forgive in a hurry, just for the sake of forgiving. Only after feeling the full force of the harm can you forgive it. It is a paradox—but then the whole idea of forgiveness is a paradox.

There's no doubt about it: sometimes anger just doesn't go away. If we have been victims of an injustice—someone has broken a promise, stolen money from us—we are full of rage and it gnaws at us, or else we express it in a destructive way. Yet it may be enough to acknowledge that, yes, we are furious, and we already feel better. Anger is no trifling matter. It is a physical reality of extraordinary intensity. Our blood boils, rancor eats away at us, we cannot digest an offense, our heart is heavy, somebody gives us a headache or is a pain in the neck—these are all common ways of speaking about the physical effects of anger. If we allow some space for it, we will feel differently; perhaps we will actively decide what to do with it. Instead of exploding or imploding, maybe we will express it in a constructive way, affirm our rights without hurting anyone, or use its energy to propel our own projects. But as long as we do not face our anger, it will remain. We cannot simply sweep it under the carpet. Kindness can find no room in us.

The other important factor (mainly in the case where we personally know the offender) is empathy with the person who has offended. If we manage to place ourselves in his shoes, understand his intentions and his suffering as well as ours, we find it easier to forgive. We can understand why he did what he did. It is no accident that the cerebral activities of forgiveness and of empathy take place in the same area of the brain.

So we will be able to forgive if we can place ourselves in another's shoes; if we are less concerned with judgment, and more with understanding; if we are humble enough to give up being the patron of justice, and flexible enough to let go of past hurts and resentments. To learn how to forgive leads us to a radical transformation of our personality.

For all these reasons, being able to forgive and being able to say sorry are two sides of the same coin—both require the same humility and flexibility. An Eastern story tells of a rigid and authoritarian king who wanted everyone to call him "Luminous and Noble Divinity." He liked the name, and wanted it. One day he discovered that there was one old man who refused to call him by that name. The king had the man brought before him and asked him why. "Not out of rebellion or lack of respect, but simply because I do not see you that way," said the old man. "It would not be sincere." For his sincerity he paid a high price. The king had him locked in an awful prison for a year, then brought the man before him once again. "Have you changed your mind?" "I am sorry, but I still do not see you that way." Another year of prison in the darkest cell, and only bread and water; he lost more weight, but did not change his mind. The king was angry, yet also curious. He decided to set him free and to follow him in secret. The old man returned to his poor fisherman's shack, where he was welcomed with great joy by his wife.

The two talked while the king listened in hiding. The woman was furious with the king for taking her husband away for two years and treating him so cruelly. But the old man was of a different mind. "He is not as bad as you think," he said. "After all, he is a good king: He has looked after the poor, built roads and hospitals, made just laws." The king was highly impressed by the words of this old man who bore him no grudge—on the contrary, he could find his virtues. The king felt a deep wave of bitter remorse. Weeping, he came out of his hiding place and stood before the man and his wife. "I owe you a great apology. Despite what I have done, you still do not hate me." The old man was surprised and said, "What I said was true, O Luminous and Noble Divinity. You are a good king."

The king was astonished. "You called me Luminous and Noble Divinity . . . why?"

"Because you were able to ask forgiveness."

Do we need to explain why the capacity to forgive is inherent in kindness? Maybe it is obvious, but let us say it anyway. We cannot be kind while we carry the weight of our resentments. Nor while we remain too rigid to ask forgiveness. Nor if our emotions are colored by guilt or vindictiveness.

We can be kind only if the past no longer dominates us.

Sometimes, however, forgiveness is impossible. Try though we may, we cannot find it in us to forgive. The offense has been too serious, the hurt too great, and forgiveness seems impossible. But there still is a way out. It is in just such a situation that we can under-stand what it truly means to forgive. It is at this point that we need to change our viewpoint. Many problems cannot be resolved at their existing level: We must learn to see them from another vantage.

For example, you are walking around town, and at a street corner someone who is running past without looking knocks you over, causing you to fall, then keeps going without even saying sorry. Any-one in that situation would be upset. But now imagine watching the scene from the top of a tower. You see two people bump into each other. But not only that. You see many other people in the town, and buildings, cars, parks, perhaps in the distance a football stadium or airport, factories, countryside. You see everything from a distance, and with a certain detachment. You see it all from another vantage point. And the accident looks different to you, far less serious, be-cause you see it in a bigger context and from farther away.

We can do the same with all our problems, hurts, obsessions, and anxieties. We can observe them from a distance. We move, as it were, to another place inside ourselves. We reach that core, a place in us where we are not hurt—where we are healthy, open, and strong. I am convinced that even those of us who have been badly hurt still possess that sound nucleus. We have just forgotten about it.

How do we find again that intact core, unpolluted by the ugliness of life, uncorrupted by compromise, not weighed down by worry, nor weakened by fear? For each of us the answer is different. Some of us reconnect with the vital, happy part of ourselves through med-itation. Others do it with physical activity. Others find their true na-ture by caring for the suffering and the needy. Yet others through beauty, or prayer, or reflection. We all have our way of reconnecting with the healthy core, our true self. And if we don't know how, we can look for a way: That is one of the most glorious adventures— perhaps *the* most glorious adventure—of our whole life.

If we can return, even for a moment, to our center, then quarrels and resentments seem an absurd waste of time to us. I have seen this change in perspective in many of my clients. When I ask them point-blank if they are willing to forgive a hurt that continues to eat into them, they may very well feel they cannot. But if I am able to help them find a place inside themselves where there is more breathing space, where love and beauty are possible, then no further effort is needed: Forgiveness is already there.

Some time ago, I was working with a man who had to look after his aging, sick, and difficult father. His four siblings had left him alone with the father, offered no help whatever, at most a bit of advice—the kind we can all do without. He was full of anger toward them, and who would blame him? As long as he and I confronted his problem the same way, no resolution appeared. So I asked him to talk to me about all that was dear to him, all that made him happy and content in his life. He liked dogs; when he spoke of them, his face lit up. He liked music. And he liked to go running. When he thought about these things, he felt better. When he went running or played with his dogs or listened to opera, he felt reborn. I asked him to re-create those states of mind. They were another part of him, cleaner and more serene. Then I asked him how, from this vantage point, he felt toward his siblings. The new perspective was totally different. No more rancor, no bitterness. On the contrary, he was grateful for all he had been able to do for his father.

Thus, if we find in ourselves the place where we feel happy and whole, forgiveness is already a fact. We do not need effort or mental acrobatics. Gone are fear, suspicion, the desire to get even. Forgiving becomes the easiest thing in the world: It is not something we do, but something we *are*. And the same goes for kindness. We don't have to do anything to be kind, because we already *are* kind.

We have only to give ourselves permission to be so.

CONTACT

To Touch and to Be Touched

The best time of our life, I suspect, is gone. This is nothing to grieve about—all of us, whatever our age, still have many possibilities for growth, challenges to overcome, occasions for fulfillment. The future can be promising, particularly if we see it this way. Yet I believe that our very best time has already passed: We reached our peak at five months of age.

It was a very brief period. Once we hit seven or eight months, much had already begun to change. At five months, however, it is a different story: A baby has mostly left behind the difficulties associated with birth; she has adapted to her new world, and life has not yet assailed her with all its hardships and contradictions. This is a moment in which fear, greed, suspicion are largely absent. The sense of time is yet undeveloped: no hurry, no anticipation, no anxiety. The baby is strong and coordinated enough to look around and connect with anyone who approaches. Sometimes you see a five-month-old baby in her mother's arms, perhaps at the post office or at friends' homes or on the bus. The baby will look at you and, though she doesn't know you, grace you with a radiant smile, a gift of happiness.

This is contact in its pure form. No one can do better. At around seven months, that baby will start experiencing stranger anxiety and will feel less comfortable with people she does not know. But at five months, the whole world is still one big family for her; each member of the family is interesting and beautiful and deserves a happy smile.

Why the mind's clock is programmed in this way remains a mystery. Why, till the age of five or six months, is every stranger a friend, and afterward, in varying degrees, caution sneaks in? Both attitudes are relevant to our survival. It is important to be able to enter into contact, and also, at times, not to trust. Sometimes the changeover is barely visible, at others it is a drama. The baby screams in the presence of anyone who is not the mother. In either case, it is a fall from a state of grace that, if we are lucky, we will be able to glimpse in future years. But it will never again be ours in quite the same way. It will never again be so spontaneous and complete.

Fortunately, some of us come close and retain a measure of this extraordinary capacity to enter into contact with anyone at all, even total strangers. In an adult, this ability takes different aspects, because an adult is independent and can speak and move at will. For some, contact happens with surprising ease. I think of Natalie, a twenty-one-year-old friend of my family. I once saw her enter a room where several others were dining. Like a ball bouncing about, Natalie cheerfully made contact with everyone. While another person might have waved a general hello to all present, she greeted each one in a unique way: with a smile, a joke, a word or reminder of a shared experience, a thought special to the person. And it all happened in seconds, naturally and spontaneously. Every person whom she touched in this way visibly changed: smiled, relaxed, felt instantly at ease.

Take another friend of mine, Judy. She is an eccentric in whom stranger anxiety appears to be totally absent. In any situation—walking down the street, standing in a crowded airport, sitting in a restaurant—she will in no time at all start a conversation with anyone, even the most diffident. One day she is standing in line at the bank. The man in front of her is contorting in an attempt to scratch his back, with little success; he cannot not reach the spot. Judy notices and offers help, "Excuse me, would you like me to scratch your back for you?" She says it without ulterior motive, without fear of adverse reaction. Most people would be too inhibited to make—or take—such an offer. It would be an intrusion into the stranger's private space. But for Judy, and for others like her, such inhibitions are absent or weaker, and the area of freedom is vaster.

How useful and important is this capacity of contact? Maybe you do not need to scratch strangers' backs at the bank. But in some measure if this faculty is alive, hitherto unknown possibilities are ignited, energy circulates, a new world is opened. And life is just more fun.

We can also do the opposite: build walls, as well as find ourselves in front of others' walls, and decide that this is an easier, more practical way to live. Let other people make a fuss. Distance may be safer. But our lives are poorer without the nourishment that these people can give—nourishment in the form of stimuli, different points of view, fresh emotions. And, as we shall see later, the fewer our contacts, the poorer our health may be.

The incapacity of being in touch with others can become a tragedy of solitude. We become our own prisoners. Why do we not succeed in opening up to others? The reasons are many, and the most common ones are that we feel inferior and other people appear to us as better and more intelligent; or we feel superior, and we think contact with others is a waste of time. Maybe we are afraid of being invaded and controlled; or perhaps we fear being humiliated and wounded.

In an old Japanese story, retold by Yasunari Kawabata, a bamboo cutter one day sees a stalk of bamboo that seems illuminated from within, and he finds there a tiny baby girl. He and his wife adopt her. In no time at all, she grows into a beautiful woman and all the men fall in love with her. But she has no desire to marry. Some suitors are particularly insistent. So she agrees to marry, on the condition that her requests be met. But the requests are impossible: for example, the bowl that the Buddha had used centuries ago, or a bejewelled branch from a tree in heaven, a dress invulnerable to flames. The suitors try trickery and are found out, or else fall by the wayside. Not even the emperor, who had fallen in love with her, succeeds. The woman remains inaccessible. Finally, it is discovered that she is not of this earth, but comes from the sublime world of the moon. She is in exile among us as punishment, to pay for a wrong she committed in a past life. Her real parents come and take her away forever. The woman is upset at having to leave her adoptive family, but then, putting on a dress of feathers, she forgets everything. To the emperor, who had tried with his soldiers to stop the moon people from taking her away, she leaves a little bottle containing the elixir of immortality. But what use is immortality without love? The emperor has the bottle of elixir taken up the highest mountain in Japan, which, ever since, has been called Fuji: the immortal.

This is the story of a failure. It is the tragedy of one who does not open herself to others and thus feels like she is from another world, makes impossible requests, distances herself from everyone. And if contact does not happen, then everything precious in the world, even the promise of immortality, loses its value.

The faculty of contact is a true talent—like musical, literary, or athletic talent. Some people are talented jugglers or mathematicians.

Some are talented in making contact with others. And like any talent, this one has two aspects. One is negative: The absence of blocks and inhibitions—everything is easy. The positive aspect is the presence of a capacity: Knowing the right way to engage, a comment that breaks the ice, body language that expresses openness and spontaneity, a laugh, a look that, without invading, touches you deeply.

I must admit that, being shy and introverted, I lack this capacity to a large extent and admire those who have it, just as I admire those with musical talent. Striking up a conversation with someone, say, on the train makes me feel somewhat insecure, and requires all my mental powers. Do I have anything interesting to say? How will the other react? Will he feel invaded? How should I proceed in the conversation? Then perhaps someone else walks in after me and starts talking as if it were the most natural thing in the world.

Recently I saw a newsagent I had not seen in two years. At one time I used to buy the newspaper from him every day. Then for two years I did not visit that town anymore. When I went back and again bought the newspaper, we said nothing to each other. Like me, he is reserved. I noted only the faintest of smiles. A look was enough to say that, yes, I had returned after two years, and we had recognized each other. We simply did not know what to say to one another, and that was okay.

Others would have transformed the situation into an opportunity to catch up and talk about health or the kids, the weather or the government. We instead kept to the minimum. But make no mistake: Introversion by itself does not prevent us from entering into contact with others. An introvert might take more time to open up and communicate, but the contact could be deeper and more lasting. Extroverts, however, do have advantages here, because they can more easily seize the possibility for contact in many situations. No doubt about it: They have more chances than the introverts.

Whether we are introverted or extroverted, an open contact is a richer and more promising way to approach our relationships. It is an attitude in which the other is seen as a window to a new world, a way for us to grow. Various are the ways in which we can grow: Creativity, for instance, or meditation, by opening ourselves to beauty through bodywork, prayer, and so on. For those with facility of contact, relationship is the main instrument of growth. Encounter with another is the field where insight and transformation occur, the avenue through which comes fulfillment.

Think of the effect meeting others has on us. Some encounters weigh on us and bore us. Afterward, we feel tired and ill-tempered. Other encounters give us energy, lift our spirits, generate new ideas. People who have the talent for contact are able to facilitate the chemistry between themselves and another person. They are able, even in the most banal and apparently insignificant of encounters, to evoke the soul.

Try this experiment. Start with an ordinary situation such as riding in a taxi, buying paper at a stationery shop, or sitting in the train. Then try exchanging a few words with the taxi driver, making eye contact with the salesperson, striking up a conversation with someone on the train. For some of us, that happens spontaneously; others have to do it deliberately. Be fully present in this brief contact, and expect the other to be so as well. Suddenly a change occurs: Something becomes unblocked and energy circulates. It might not be an encounter of two souls. But it surely will be an exchange of vital energy between two people.

Maybe in this simple operation we will face our internal blocks, inhibitions that have been with us since childhood. These are deep, long-term inhibitions, which sometimes have damaging results. For example, research shows that if parents inculcate in their children fear and suspicion of strangers, the children have greater difficulty as adolescents with their peer relations.

In encounters with another, we often use some reassuring prop: to be well dressed, for example, or to have an impressive professional role, or to be in touch with an important person, or to have in hand the latest model cell phone. Such aids reassure us and might appear to facilitate interactions, but in fact they reduce its quality. They distract us from what really counts.

Why then do we use them? Because most of us are afraid. Just think of a time at a party or meeting when you have entered a room full of strangers and no one made the introductions. In the contact with another, we feel naked. We are exposed, defenseless. All we have is our being. We put ourselves on the line, which, however uncomfortable, is just what facilitates the contact. Because we don't know what might happen, we are slightly or greatly intimidated. Contact with another can be terrifying, so we protect ourselves with roles, masks, and other props.

Particular situations, because they eliminate all that is superfluous, make contact truer and more intense. Sex, for instance, is contact par excellence. At its best, two bodies intertwine and two souls join as one. But the sexual encounter can also exemplify *non*-contact. Two bodies move and touch, but the two souls remain distracted and estranged.

Sometimes conflict itself creates the conditions for contact. My wife, Vivien, has a special habit of making friends with those who treat her rudely or arrogantly. She may be in a shop or with a salesperson or with a parent of one of our kids' classmates, and become the victim of a small injustice: someone pushing in front of her in a line, or trying to sell her something she does not want, or speaking impolitely to her. She does not start arguing. Rather, with benevolent doggedness, she will try to strike up a conversation, establish contact, but never mention the wrong. She will talk about the kids, or joke, or ask an opinion, or comment on the weather. And she will not let up till she sees an opening—some sign of interest, a word, a smile.

I asked Vivien why she does this. "I have never wanted enemies," she answered. "And I am a big believer in redemption."

DEATH, TOO, CAN BE A MOMENT OF CONTACT. DEATH IS DE-finitive. We know that afterward, no more contact is possible. A person is going away forever: It's goodbye, the last chance to tell her we love her. We know we will never see her again, never be able to confide in her again, or laugh and joke together again. When nothing interferes with death, a contact full of pathos is possible, a freeing of feelings and intuitions. Pain opens us. It does away with all that is inessential or superficial. An empty new space allows real contact.

Extreme situations, too, like hunger, thirst, poverty, imprisonment, danger, and war can unexpectedly unite two people. These are situations in which the rules of the game have changed. Something that before had value, like social role, no longer counts. A famous example is the encounter between Primo Levi and another inmate of a concentration camp. In that terrible and desolate world, the two men speak about *The Divine Comedy*, and for a moment transcend the inhuman condition in which they are constrained. Levi explains to his prisonmate the verses of Ulysses from Dante's *Inferno*. He remembers the passage with difficulty, and finds it hard to translate it into French, but still the beauty of the poetry is the means by which these two men meet, have contact.

Music is yet another facilitator of contact. Here, too, inhibitions and social rules are canceled or at least relaxed while people enjoy beauty. Many years ago, I was lucky enough to attend a private concert by the great Indian musician Ravi Shankar. I had heard that he had a sore throat; and when I saw him just before the concert started, he indeed looked out of sorts. Then he and his ensemble began playing. During the music, I noticed that in the very brief pauses between phrases, the musicians would look at one another. It was an intense look, for the purpose of synchronizing rhythm, but also, I am sure, for synchronizing souls. It was visible and apparent that those musicians were meeting at that moment in a timeless realm. Their encounter, real and tangible before everyone's eyes, was full of happiness. At the end of the concert, Shankar was radiant.

DOUBTLESS, THE CAPACITY FOR CONTACT HAS A DETERMINing influence on health. People with greater capacity for contact have a bigger and better network of social support than those less able to establish relationships with others. One study directly measured individuals' sociability in relation to the efficiency of their immune system. Questionnaires and interviews given to 334 people examined their sociability—the quantity and quality of their relationships in everyday life. These people were then exposed to a common cold virus, and it was found that the more sociable a person was, the less susceptible he was to contagion. This finding was independent of age, emotional style, stress, and habits regarding maintenance of health, such as physical exercise or vitamin pills.

You can see just how important contact is when you study what happens in its absence or insufficiency. Social isolation and its effects on the organism have been studied since at least the 1970s. The main findings indicate that lack of contact is linked to various illnesses and a shorter life expectancy. It is considered by many as serious a health hazard as smoking. Social isolation correlates with a greater incidence of cardiac disease, sleep disturbance, depression, backache, deterioration of memory—especially in the elderly, for whom the lack of stimuli is lethal.

Facility of contact is a basic aspect of kindness. Where you find contact, you find the heart. You find an attitude that makes you feel that this person is right there, just for you. That you are her or his priority at that moment. That you count.

Without contact between two people, everything becomes gray and automatic. Individuals interacting resemble robots more than human beings. Their dealings are without substance; and kindness—if we can call it that—is an exterior politeness, an empty, heartless ritual. Contact is a door through which kindness can flow.

The fabric of our society is made of the contacts each person has with others. These contacts multiply to form a web. There are many analogies to these webs: electrical circuits, neural connections in the brain of mammals, chemical reactions in a cell, the ramifications of the Internet, and the ecosystem of the planet. They are complex relations in which every element is important. However isolated we may feel, we are still in relation to millions of other people.

In the famous study on degrees of separation by Stanley Milgram, it was found that when we discover a friend or relation in common with a person we have encountered by chance, it is not a rare coincidence but rather the rule. We really are in a tighter network and closer communication with everybody than we can imagine. And we influence others far more than we think and they know. By changing others' states of mind, we propagate ourselves in countless ways. Right in the midst of everyday life we are given the chance to touch the lives of others and thus change the world.

SENSE OF BELONGING

I Belong, Therefore I Am

Because I live in the country, I have to drive along a few back-roads before I reach the highway that takes me to work. These tranquil roads are often a little slow. One beautiful summer morning, I find myself behind a man on a tractor. Every twenty or thirty meters, he stops to chat with someone. I cannot overtake him on such a narrow, winding road. The conversations only take a few seconds—the time to say hello and exchange news—but they are enough to make me nervous. I do not know what he could be talking about with the people he meets at the roadside, but clearly it is nothing urgent. And here am I behind him, in a hurry to get to work, fuming as I wait for this man to finish his conversation. I cannot toot the horn (here that would be considered rude—or an act of lunacy). All I can do is wait, and churn out angry thoughts.

Then suddenly I realize what is going on: It is not anger I feel, but envy. This person in front of me, with the calm pace of the peasant, has something that I, rushing commuter that I am, do not have: besides a tranquillity that sharply contrasts with my haste, he has also the privilege—given mainly to those born in the country—of belonging to a local web of relationships with parents, aunts and uncles, children, cousins, friends . . . all bound to the same customs, not merely for one lifetime but for generations. They all know each other, through fortune and misfortune, hopes and disappointments. I, having arrived a few years ago from the city, do not have this, and though I am always greeted with courtesy, I do not feel I really belong to the place. It is the difference between, on the one hand, a centuries-old oak with roots deep and wide that interweave with other roots and know the soil in which they thrive and, on the other hand, a recently transplanted exotic sapling. The man who stopped every few meters was not being discourteous toward me, he was simply affirming the vitality of his connections. He was affirming his sense of belonging.

The sense of belonging is a basic need and at the same time the answer to a question. We ask ourselves: What am I part of? And this question resembles—perhaps coincides with—another equally crucial question: Who am I? We belong to a family, a group, a society, a professional category; and the affiliations define us and give us reasons for existing. Without this belonging, we would feel like nothing. It is hard, maybe impossible, to know who we are without some reference to others. That is why the sense of belonging is a basic need, like the need for food, water, or a roof over our heads.

We may hear ourselves object, "You have to learn to stand alone, be independent!" And yet the urge to belong comes first. The extraordinary intensity of this need probably comes from our ancestral past, when the only way to stay alive was to be part of a group. No one could manage alone. Even today, in our precarious and sometimes threatening world, where we are exposed to innumerable dangers, with sickness and old age lying in wait for us, we need the protection and security that only other human beings can offer.

For many, the sense of belonging is maintained and reinforced by small rituals that punctuate the day.

I stop at the gas station to fill up. A man passes and says to the attendant, "Giovanni, what do you say, is it going to rain or not?" "No way." And that's it. What is the function of this interchange? Certainly not merely to exchange meteorological information. It seems pointless, if not inane. Yet it is a vital exchange because it serves to circulate energy and reaffirm those two people's sense of belonging. A brief chat at the bar or the newsstand, a chance meeting on the street, a few words at the bank, a wave from the car, getting together for coffee at work, waiting for the children to get out of school—all these little rituals revitalize the sense of being part of a community, they comfort and reassure us even if we do not even realize it. It is easier in small towns and villages where everybody knows each other, harder in cities. The weekend may emphasize either belonging or solitude: those with a strong support network are fine, others risk the Sunday blues.

IN MY WORK AS A PSYCHOTHERAPIST, I OFTEN SEE HOW THE sense of belonging has been wounded, or has not had the chance to develop—first of all in the family, where we learn to feel part of an entity that, ideally, should protect and nurture us; and later at school, among friends, at work. When the need for belonging is not met, discomfort arises, including feelings of depression, disorientation, and hostility.

More than in any other time in human history, the sense of belonging has recently been denied by newly adopted habits, and by social and technological innovations. These are things that make everyday life perhaps smoother and more practical, but also colder. Profit and efficiency win over warmth and rapport. A small example: Until recently, I used to go to a particular fruit vendor in a little town near my home to buy marinated artichokes. They were delicious. Moreover, I knew they were hand-selected by the vendor, because he spoke of them with the pride of the shopkeeper who chooses only the best. Every now and then we would exchange a few words. One day I went to the shop but found it closed. Through the glass I saw an empty store, cardboard strewn on the floor: The typical sad scene of places closed down—a business that is no longer. I slowly came to understand what had happened: The artichoke man had closed up shop because of the new nearby supermarket, a grandiose complex that has devastated the original structure of the small town and forced the traffic into hyperkinetic paths. Thus I found myself at the supermarket, standing in front of twenty different brands of marinated artichokes. Maybe my brand was there, too, but I was no longer in the mood. I pushed the grocery cart in line along with the others, to the sound of the cash registers, in an environment where I know I am part of a predictable and calculated flow of clients. My world had just become colder.

The situation is made more complex by another important factor: We live in an era of individualism. The individual is celebrated in every form. To be special and creative, to offer an original contribution, to compete with others and be the best: Nowadays this is a guiding idea for many people. It is also a criterion for judging and admiring others, and a value on which we model our own lives. It was not always like this. In other eras and civilizations, individuality was less important; perhaps it was not even possible to conceive it as we do today.

Art history clearly shows us this development. In medieval Europe, the art was full of sacred themes and served, for the most part, as a means of educating the illiterate: paintings and sculptures usually depict episodes from the Bible.

Then comes the breakthrough: Almost overnight, at the beginning of the Renaissance, canvases and frescoes begin to feature contemporary human personages. These pieces of art celebrated the beauty of a human being, and his or her dignity and creative potential. Now what counts is the splendor of the individual.

It is a new paradigm, which multiplies human possibilities. What can you, unique individual, do with all your talents and qualities? No one had ever thought explicitly about it. It was an extraordinary idea that gave rise to countless discoveries and victories. These revolutions in thought took centuries to be assimilated and become part of our culture, but now they are our common heritage, and they appear even in cheap and commercialized form.

This elevation of individuality is certainly at the base of an extraordinary period of progress for humanity. But it has exacted a high price: Our egos are inflated and we have neglected our community, our feeling part of a human environment in harmony with us. In our contemporary epoch, we oscillate between two poles—the uniformity and anonymity of the masses, and the fascination of individual originality. The importance of belonging to a community is often forgotten.

A JEWISH TALE TELLS OF A GOOD KING WHO IS DYING. BEfore all his weeping subjects, he calls for someone to bring him an arrow and asks the weakest of them to break it. The man does so with ease. Then he asks for a bundle of arrows bound together and asks the strongest of them to break it. Despite all his efforts, the man cannot do it. To his subjects he says, "As my inheritance, I bequeath to you the union among you all. Be united with one another. This oneness will give you great strength, which alone you would never be able to attain."

The sense of belonging—that is, the feeling that we are part of a whole greater than ourselves, with which we are physically, mentally, and spiritually involved—is a necessary factor to our well-being. Furthermore, when we feel isolated, we will seek some affiliation at all costs, even with groups that are violent, dangerous, extremist. This is one of the reasons many adolescents are attracted by gangs, cults, and sects. The typical profile of a young person at risk includes confusion of identity, alienation from the family, weak links with the community, feelings of impotence, and an unfulfilled need for belonging. If you grow up without truly being included by family or school or the society in which you live, you will feel the need to be important to other human beings whom you recognize as similar to you, and who in turn recognize you as similar to them. That is the way into a cult, and it can be hard to find the way out.

Unless we have always been monstrously popular, all of us have in our history some episode in which we experienced exclusion: No one wanted to play with us when we were kids, or we were not invited to a party, or we were left off the soccer team. My most vivid recollection of exclusion is from my senior high school years. The teacher was assigning topics for research that was to be carried out in pairs or groups. The other students were choosing topics and partners for this task. It soon became obvious that no one wanted to work with me. There was a moment of icy silence in which I felt like a fragment lost in space and without contacts. Then one of my classmates, Guido, offered to work with me, and saved the day. What immense relief!

Did he step forward purely out of sympathy, or because he really wanted to be my partner? It did not really matter. I was safe because, however imperfectly, I too belonged.

So: being part of a group or a community gives many benefits. It makes us feel recognized, allows us to interact with others, defeats the terrible specter of loneliness. Yet it often exacts a toll—we have to conform to the culture of that group, to its predominant ideas, its lifestyle, its way of dressing, speaking, eating, its preferences in music, sport, and so on. In some cases, the toll is heavy: Belonging to a group may oppress spontaneity and freedom of expression. The dangers are many—conformity, discrimination against those outside the group, and a false euphoria, based not on real strength, but only on the security of belonging.

Akin to the sense of belonging is the sense of support—the confidence of receiving help by the community when in need. The two are similar, but with support, the accent is on the practical possibility of receiving help from others rather than on the feeling of being included. Sometimes support and belonging are treated as synonyms. Research has found that support is extraordinarily important for physical and mental health. The greater the number of friends upon whom we can count, and the better the quality of these relationships, the greater is our longevity and our health. Many studies have demonstrated this fact; the book *Love and Survival* by Dean Ornish treats it thoroughly. I will cite only a few examples. In Sweden, some 18,000 men and women were followed over a period of six years. Those who felt most isolated were four times more at risk of dying prematurely than were the others. In a Finnish study, more than 13,000 people were studied. Those who felt more connected to the community had two to three times less risk of dying prematurely than those who were isolated. The Tecumseh study of almost 3,000 people found that when the feeling of support is less, the frequency of illness (heart attacks, strokes, cancer, arthritis, and lung disease) increases two to three times. In Dr. Redford Williams's study of 1,400 people with cardiac disease, those who were married or had someone in whom they could confide had a two to three times greater chance of surviving the disease.

Sometimes being alone can be a relief and can give us a feeling of freedom and spaciousness. True loneliness—cosmic loneliness—is different. It is the feeling that whatever happens to us has not the tiniest importance to anyone else; that what we think or say will never be heard with interest by anyone else, and that we do not mean anything to anyone. It is the feeling that if we ceased to exist, everything would continue as before and no one would notice.

Does the sense of belonging depend only on the objective situation, or can it change and be developed in difficult situations—loneliness, anonymity, and so on? I lean toward the second hypothesis. Each one of us feels a sense of belonging in certain groups—but how flexible are we, and how much variety can we manage? Will I feel I belong only when I am at the bridge club, or only when I hang out with Caucasian people, or with devotees of my religion, or with fans of my team—and in no other situation? Or will I feel I have something in common with others wherever I am? And will my sense of belonging extend even to animals, places, and entire populations?

Although the feeling of belonging is usually taken to be dependent on the local ties of an individual, maybe the ability to feel part of an ever larger community can be cultivated. I remember when, at the beginning of my career, I used to go abroad to teach in various European countries, it was often an upsetting experience for me. I would feel culture shock nearly every time. I was painfully aware of the difference in rhythm, style, language, and mentality, even though I was going to countries within the European tradition. I would always feel I had to adapt to some custom or other, and it seemed a gigantic task. I was exhausted after every workshop.

I recall my astonishment at one of my colleagues, more experienced and established than me, who for years had been traveling the world with great ease, working a weekend in Japan, the next one in

Australia, a week later in Finland, then perhaps in Israel. From all this movement, instead of exhaustion, she would derive renewed energy and vitality. How did she do it? I told her that I felt the cultural diversity of the participants in my workshops as an ordeal. I still remember her brief and enlightening reply: "They are all people like us, you know."

There you have a sense of belonging that is refined, and above all free and active in any situation. Some spiritual traditions have recognized the importance of this openness. Christianity, for example, talks about seeing in every individual our brother or sister. Tibetan Buddhism invites us to carry out a curious mental exercise: to look at whomever we meet as someone who, in a previous life, of the infinite series of incarnations through which we have passed, has been our mother. If we think that this person, who perhaps feels like a stranger to us, this rude driver, this loud-mouthed hooligan, this inattentive saleswoman or lazy waiter, if we think that this person in a past life was our mother, that she nurtured and raised us, tended our wounds and endured our tantrums and washed our clothes and stroked our heads, in one of our innumerable lives in who knows what remote situation, then that person is no longer a stranger, but part of one immense family in which we have the privilege to belong.

Thus our sense of belonging can be rigid and rusty—and can be restricted to a tight circle. Or it can be free, flexible, and active even in the toughest situations, making life easier and more pleasing. It seems evident to me that these attitudes have to do with kindness. If I see you as different and I view you with suspicion, or at the best with cold neutrality, it is unlikely that I will feel kindly disposed toward you. If instead I look at you knowing we both belong to the human race, both have a similar nature, different experiences but the same roots and a common destiny, then it is probable I will feel openness, solidarity, empathy toward you. In other words, kindness.

And just as it is possible to modulate our own sense of belonging, so it is possible to influence that sense in others. We can make others feel included or excluded, and in different ways: by our words, our glances, our body language in general.

I recall one day many years ago when, at a conference, I had to speak on a panel with several illustrious experts. I was at the beginning of my career, rather intimidated, and seated at one end of a panel of four or five bigwigs, all of us facing the audience. Each had to give a short talk, then we would have a discussion. The man next to me, a famous university professor, from the start turned a full ninety degrees and sat with his back to me the whole time, paying attention only to his colleagues. It did not bother me—it was too comical to hurt. I realized, however, how easy it is to physically exclude or include a person just through our posture.

Luckily, we can also act in the opposite way to that of the haughty professor. Opportunities for helping others feel included come along regularly. We are all referees and players in this sport. We can cultivate our sense of belonging, and decide to include others or not.

It is all a question of how kind we want to be.

TRUST

Are You Willing to Risk?

I found myself one day in the magical city of Istanbul (though this story could have happened anywhere). At that time, I was a young philosophy student and not yet wise to the dirty devices of the world. A friendly, pleasant man approached me and offered to change my money at a very favorable rate. I agreed. He took the money and asked me to wait on the street corner. Only after I had waited a long time did I understand that he had no intention of returning with the promised sum. Come to think of it, he had left in a hurry, and quickly disappeared in the maze of the old town.

Yes, I had been incredibly naive. But do we have to jump to the conclusion that we live in a world of liars and thieves, that we cannot trust anybody? To trust is a bet. Each time we trust, we put ourselves on the line. If we confide in a friend, we can be betrayed. If we have faith in a partner, we can be abandoned. If we trust in the world, we can be crushed. Far too often it ends that way. But the alternative is worse still, because if we do not put ourselves on the line, nothing will happen.

Thus, whether we are aware of it or not, every act of trust carries with it a shiver of fear. A favorable situation can become dangerous. Deep down we know that life is insecure and precarious. However, if we do trust, the shiver carries with it a philosophical optimism: Life, with all its traps and horrors, is good.

The bet is implicit in trust itself. If we could be sure of everyone and everything, trust would have no value—like money, if it were suddenly limitless, or sunshine, if there were always fine weather, or life, if we were to live forever. Yet we know that in giving our trust, we can be cheated, even thwarted. Trust is costly. How ready are we to pay?

EMILIO, MY ELEVEN-YEAR-OLD SON, HAS ASKED PERMIS-sion to make pancakes. Immediately I imagine burns, flour all over the floor, tears—not to mention inedible pancakes. Yet seeing the hope and enthusiasm in his eyes, I let him do it. After a while I go to the kitchen, where I find no disasters—just neatly stacked pancakes. Emilio is proud of his work, and the pancakes are tasty. This is how trust works: It produces not only pancakes, but also satisfaction and independence, while a vote of no confidence ("Only grown-ups can make pancakes") produces frustration and paralysis.

Another example, this time the opposite: I once had a psychotherapy client who was a kleptomaniac. She held a prestigious position, yet had an irresistible desire to shoplift. When she thought no one was looking, she would steal—a pen, a book, a pair of scissors—and hide the item in her handbag. The operation was always accompanied by anxiety. What would have happened if she, well known, were caught? Catastrophe. But as soon as she was out of the shop, she would feel exhilarated and triumphant. In working with me, she understood that her compulsive desire to steal was a rebel-

lion against lack of trust, for in the house where she grew up, everything was under lock and key, and each family member distrusted
all the others. No one left anything lying around, the house was always impeccably tidy—and depressingly empty. The locked cabi-
nets continually told her "We do not trust you. We are afraid you
will steal. You are dishonest." Thus she had started to steal.

Distrust can have profound and lasting effects on our personalities—disparaging and destructive effects. Trust produces the
opposite: It aids and nourishes us, and it multiplies our possibilities.
Trust, along with warmth, is perhaps the quality whose origins go
back furthest in our evolutionary history. It is a mammalian—and
especially a human—characteristic. Our survival is linked to trust.
Think of a baby, asleep in its mother's arms, in perfect surrender.
The baby seems fashioned to be cradled in arms, which in turn are
made to measure for him. In the very first year of life, we will either
have basic trust, which will then accompany our every step, or else
distrust, which will burden us with fear and anger throughout our
lives. Being the species most dependent and for the longest time, we
entrust ourselves to the prolonged care and protection of our parents. And it is thanks to this prolonged dependence that for many
years we need not worry about our survival, but are free to play and
learn more than any other species. Trust is inherent in our biology.

Perhaps it is this biological component that links trust to good
health, for research has found that people with greater trust are generally healthier. If you wake up in the morning with the thought of
having to defend yourself, with the fear that something bad might
happen to you or your family, you will be worse off than if you regard the world as a welcoming place. In a sample of a hundred men
and women between the ages of fifty-five and eighty, it was found
that those more trusting had better health and greater satisfaction in
their lives. In a follow-up study fourteen years later, the more trust-

ing ones were also found to be longer-lived. The researchers' conclusions were that trust has a protective effect on our health. In another study, carried out on university students, the more trusting were found to have a greater degree of humor.

And what about the business world? One would think that caution, rather than trust, would be the rule here. And yet a number of studies have asked the question, Do businesses that are rich in trust succeed more than those that are not? The conclusions are always the same: Businesses function better where trust is the norm. How could it be otherwise? In what kind of situation are we more likely to work better? In one where everyone suspects everyone else, and interprets with suspicion every action, word, expression? Or in a group of people ready to be friendly and united?

Trust in clients makes for good business. Muhammad Yunus, the founder of the Grameen Bank in Bangladesh, gives loans to the very poor, helping them to start small businesses such as an umbrella or boat factory, fly-screen manufacture, spice or cosmetic industry. There are no laws applying to the loans, no guarantee is required—the clients would not be able to pay anyway—and no written contract, just their word. Yunus has great faith in the latent resources of all human beings. The results bear him out because, with his faith, he has helped thousands of people emerge from poverty and rise to the dignity of independent means. This is good business, not charity: the repayment of his loans is ninety-nine percent—higher than the repayment by rich clients with regular banks.

Trust has a way of relaxing inhibitions and resolving past trauma—another possible reason for its wholesome effect. The fears, doubts, and suspicions we carry not only block our actions, they erode our energy. If a substantial part of our mental effort is spent in worry and self-defense, what becomes of our potential to take new initiatives, to create something original, or to enjoy life?

Even caution, a necessary attitude in our survival, can in large doses stop or delay us.

To place trust in someone is like giving a gift. When I trust my six-year-old son Jonathan to bring me a cup of coffee without spilling it, when I lend a favorite book to a colleague and count on his returning it, when I confide a secret to a friend, knowing he could tell others, I am giving the gift of trust, I am saying to these people: "You can do it; you are trustworthy." The gift of trust is a statement about our relationship. It empowers the other person and expands his or her possibilities.

We have seen that risk is implicit in trust. In placing trust in someone, I make myself vulnerable. The confidence might be betrayed, the coffee might be spilled on the carpet, and the book might be lost forever. But it is just this vulnerability that gives trust its value. For if trust were secure, it would become bureaucracy. It is because we put ourselves on the line that trust is so warm and precious.

What if I do not let Jonathan bring me the coffee? Or do not lend the book? Or do not confide the secret? It could be a wise choice, but I will be subtracting a possibility from the lives of those people, and perhaps diminishing their own confidence in themselves. I will also be distancing myself from them, for I will feel much closer to my son or to a friend if I have confidence in him, participate in his life, identify with him.

I watch Jonathan cross the room, cup of coffee in his hands, ready to offer it to a guest. He is distracted for a moment, wobbles, almost trips on the rug. The liquid in the cup swills dangerously. He just might spill it, scald himself, drop the cup in the guest's lap. But no, the cup arrives safely at its destination. I have had faith in him and risked. In this way I am with him, I become part of him while he is involved in his adventure. Distrust sets up a distance, perhaps a barrier. Trust creates intimacy.

Thus we have two opposite views of the world. In one, we would like everything to be secure and predictable. In the other, we accept insecurity as part of life, and we know that to seek absolute security is folly. Many traditional tales tell of powerful kings who feel in danger—they know someone will overthrow them. They try to defend themselves, but despite all their power, they fail because no one is invulnerable. Every Achilles has his heel.

In the one worldview, we distance ourselves from others by suspicion; in the other, we draw nearer to them. We understand that our destiny is linked to theirs. In the one view, we are pessimists, shielding ourselves from attack, deception, theft, and other evils. The alarm system is switched on at all times. In the other, we are more optimistic about our relations with others and we see insecurity as a source of novelty and interest.

We can read the world both ways. A stranger is approaching you in the street. How do you perceive him? A waste of time, a nuisance wanting to sell you a useless trinket, or maybe a delinquent? The alarm rings. You think of what you are going to say, how to avoid him or defend yourself. You feel tense, perhaps afraid. He walks toward you with determined step. He looks threatening. But no, he just wanted to give you the keys you dropped while getting out of the car. The alarm switches off.

For how long do we keep the alarm turned on? The alarm and defense systems we see around us are metaphors of our mental processes. The video cameras filming our every public movement; the remote-controlled gates that seem to say, "Stop! Who are you?"; the customs officials who open our baggage and the police dogs that sniff them; the electronic checkout systems in shops, making sure we haven't stolen anything; the steel-reinforced doors with special locks; the machines to check banknotes; the alarms that go off even when there is no robber; the security gates at airports; the helicopters surveying the city; barbed wire; guard dogs with their menacing bark when you walk past—these defenses, necessary as they may be, intimidate us and make us feel anxious and uneasy.

This kind of apparatus, human, animal, or mechanical, is nothing other than our fears materialized. Those spying devices, barriers, locks, before they were created were first formed inside us. We use and maintain them day after day, invest our energy in order to make them function. And we continue to make them function even when there is no more need for them.

We could also drop our guard. I once went into a restaurant where there was no cashier. You finished your meal, opened the cash box, and put in what you owed, taking change if necessary. What a treat to be trusted like that! The food tasted ever so much better. A few years later I returned and could not find that restaurant anymore—there was an insurance company instead. Perhaps they had been too trusting. So how do we know whether to trust or not?

A recent study found that high-trusters are not naive, but rather have an intelligence that permits them to distinguish between the trustworthy and the untrustworthy. The low-trusters do not trust others because they do not have this capacity, and play it safe by saying no to everyone. Their social life is poorer. Obviously, a certain degree of suspicion is healthy and wise. But when it forms part of our character, becomes our worldview and turns into muscular tension, then it becomes a hindrance.

Trust and kindness go hand in hand. Kindness is trusting and ready to risk; it brings us close to others. To trust is to be kind to others. How do we feel toward someone who seems kind at first, but when called into question does not have faith in us? His kindness has no substance—it is soulless courtesy. And how do we feel, instead, when someone has more faith in us than we have in ourselves? We feel uplifted, because that faith helps us discover in ourselves a trait or ability we perhaps did not know we had. Not only that: Trust is the soul itself of a successful relationship. My friend John Whitmore, a business consultant who leads an impressive number of workshops and conferences, has asked many people the same question: Which relationship in your life has nourished and encouraged you most and why? In almost all cases the response is the same: It was a relationship where they felt trusted.

A study looked at the effects of trust in a group of thirty-two adults who had survived the terrible Hurricane Iniki, which struck the Hawaiian island of Kauai on September 11, 1992. These people were asked, "How did trust in yourself, in others, or in God influence your life during and after the hurricane?" The subjects, from eight different ethnic groups, answered that trust had a positive influence in various areas, such as gratitude, responsibility, and mutual support. According to the researchers, trust increased the self-esteem of the survivors and improved their relationships with family and friends. The greatest benefit was a decrease in fear and an increase in sense of security, which in turn helped the subjects reach safety.

Another research study examined the change in several people after accidents that had caused them serious injuries. How had trauma transformed them? The research showed that their faith in other human beings had increased, precisely because the subjects were immobilized and powerless, had to place their care in others' hands, and had so much less control over their movements and their lives. It is hard to know what goes on in the mind of someone who has had a grave accident. But one thing is certain: Her situation is changed, and she is no longer in control. She just has to surrender.

At the center of trust we find surrender. The ability to let go has a profound and revolutionary effect on us. We realize that we cannot control everything, that we might as well abandon certainty—or the illusion of certainty—and that we can let ourselves go, accepting what life brings us. The change consists in the loosening of tension. Letting go is a major spiritual breakthrough. We can find it in trust, but also in other attitudes such as forgiveness and love. We can also find it in the face of a seemingly insoluble problem. We give up, and by some benevolent paradox, that very attitude releases the solution. Some form of understanding often follows self-surrender—it is a process we see in artistic creation, in prayer, in scientific reflection, in meditation.

A Tibetan story tells of an earnest man seeking enlightenment. A sage passes through his village and the man asks the sage to teach him the art of meditation. The sage explains: Withdraw from the world, meditate every day in such and such a way, and you will attain enlightenment. The earnest man goes to live in a cave and follows the instructions. Time passes—but no enlightenment. Two years, five, ten, twenty pass. After so many years, the sage happens once again in that village. The earnest man meets him and recounts that, despite all his efforts, he did not manage to achieve enlightenment. The sage asks, "What type of meditation did I teach you?" The man tells him. The sage: "Oh, what a terrible mistake I made! That was not the right meditation for you. You should have done another one, completely different. But now it is too late."

Disconsolate, the man returns to his cave. He has lost all hope, abandoned every wish, effort, and attempt at control. He does not know what to do. So he does what he is best at: He starts meditating. And soon enough, to his great surprise, confusion dissolves and a marvelous inner world reveals itself to him. He feels light, regenerated. In a moment of spiritual ecstasy he attains enlightenment. When, in his happy state, he leaves the cave, he sees the world around him transfigured: the snowy peaks, the pure air, the blue sky, the shining sun. He is happy. He knows he has reached the goal. And in the beauty of the enchanted scene he thinks he can see the benevolent smile of the sage.

Why did this man succeed just when he stopped trying? Because he could let himself go. The Indian mystic Ramakrishna used to say that we must be like a leaf that has fallen from a tree and is whirling in the air, without any reference point. Trusting, we let ourselves go. We know we cannot have total control. Perhaps for a moment we panic, then the tension dissipates and we are free.

In trusting, we let ourselves go. We know that all kinds of unexpected events may come our way. Our tension eases, our mind and our heart open spontaneously to new possibilities. It is an ever-new state of mind, in the present moment, because we have detached from all we know. But it is also a feeling as old as can be, because, before all betrayals and all disappointments, there was a time in which trusting another was the very substance of our life.

MINDFULNESS

The Only Time Is Now

In a Taoist story, a middle-aged man has lost his mind. He forgets everything. At night, he can no longer remember what he did during the day. And the next day, he cannot recall the evening before. At home, he forgets to sit down, and on the street, he forgets to walk. At every moment his mind erases what has happened the moment before.

His relatives are desperate. They try everything—doctors, sorcerers, shamans—but nothing works. In the end, Confucius comes, and says, "I know what the problem is. I have a secret medicine. Leave me alone with him." They do as he asks. The cure takes some time, and no one knows what is happening. At the end, the man recovers his memory.

He is cured, but furious. "Before, when I forgot everything, my mind was pure and free. Now it is weighed down with memories: Decades of successes and failures, losses and gains, pleasure and pain. And because I remember the past, I am worried about the future.

"I felt much better before. Give me back my forgetfulness!"

There you are: Think about the past or anticipate the future, and you are no longer present but immersed in the flow of time. And time, we find out, is the great mystery. Just thinking about it makes our head spin. Our whole life—birth, childhood, first day of school, adolescence, friendships, loves, work, the milestones of our existence—can seem like a very long span, full of countless events. Or else it can seem to have passed all too quickly. Think of one year, the one just passed. A year can contain a thousand happenings, pleasant and unpleasant, and it too can seem long or brief, or long and brief at once. Then think of one hour. How much can happen in one hour! Then think of one minute. Even in one minute, a thousand thoughts crowd into our minds. It can seem interminable, but it is over in a flash. Now think of one second. We say the word, and it has passed. But where is the fleeting moment? Is it briefer than a second? Than a tenth of a second? A thousandth of a second? However brief it may be, it cannot be the present, because it is already past, or else it has not yet come. The present is intangible.

That intangible moment is all that we really have, all we really are. The past is already lost. The future, however promising, is still a fairy tale. Only the present *is*—and we cannot grasp it. Yet we are always *in* the present. There is no moment in which we are not in the present. The present actually never escapes us, because we are eternally immersed in it.

We can only escape the present with our minds. Sometimes this is a boon. Memories can nourish and strengthen us. As we will see in the chapter on memory, our history travels with us, and if we did not have a past, we would not have a future. One of the most terrible symptoms of senile dementia is amnesia: The sufferer is in the present, but a present without history, and therefore she does not know who she is, and what has happened up to that moment. She is an orphan of her own history.

The past, our past, is our own heritage. But it can remove us from the present. If our past contains happy moments and we insist on recreating them, we will be out of phase, because the present is different. We do not realize that everything has changed. We will be obsolete without knowing it. If, on the other hand, our past is full of darkness and trauma, then it is a nightmare from which we try to flee. But this past can be so strong as to follow us and take over the present by force—at least till we learn to live truly in the here and now. So the man in the Chinese story is right after all. His paradox reminds us that we can be free only if we live fully in the present.

We can also be projected into the future. This state is, to some degree, positive. The future is that to which we can still give shape. It is the dominion of potential, thus full of hope and creativity. Without a future, without a project, we are not really human. But to live in the future is to be in a place that does not yet exist. The future can be seen as positive, but also as a danger. It can weigh on us—be a time to which we do not want to go. But we know we will get there anyway, no matter how hard we put on the brakes. It can also be a time full of things to do; just thinking about it can exhaust us, knowing we will never manage to do them all. And this stress prevents us from being fully in the one moment in which we really could do something: the present.

The forgetful man in the Chinese story is furious because he has found the past but lost the present. Luckily, in real life we can find the present again and again. This is a simple recipe available to everybody: Do what you are doing. Indeed, it is an ancient recipe for fleeing all evil: *Age quod agis.* If I am doing what I am doing, without fantasies of approaching dangers, without my mind displaced, I am centered. I am here one hundred percent. If so, then in that moment I am afraid of nothing, and need nothing. Thus I find fullness.

I have seen how mindfulness can almost instantly change an in-

dividual or a group of people when I observed a friend, Andrea Bocconi, a psychologist with Buddhist leanings, leading a group in a
walking meditation. Andrea was instructing the students in mindfulness. The participants had to walk up and down slowly, paying
attention to each step: now my right foot is touching the ground,
now I am raising my left foot, and so on. In just five minutes, the
atmosphere in the group changed, from being distracted and dis-
persed to being clear and open. I wondered what might happen if
world parliaments, or the board of directors in large businesses,
were to start their working day in the same way. For Buddhism, a
mindful life is the path to liberation. But just a bit of attention can
carry us a long way.

Meditative techniques based on attention in the present moment
have been used clinically with excellent therapeutic results (for instance, in order to deal with anxiety, skin disorders, or chronic pain).
You learn to be in the present, observing everything as it is, without
judging, adding, or subtracting. What is, is—let us not superimpose
any labels or judgments. Moreover, paying attention is health-
giving. In an experiment with two groups of elderly people, one
group was given plants to look after and had more chances to make
choices during the day; in other words, they had to pay attention in
the present moment. The other group carried along in their usual
way, without any instruction. After a year, the number of deaths in
the mindful group, as compared with the other group, was less than
half. The lesson is literal: Be mindful and you will be alive.

BY BEING MORE ATTENTIVE, YOU ARE ALSO LUCKIER. HOW
come some people always seem to be lucky, and all the coincidences
go their way? Is it just chance, or is there another reason? An English
psychologist, Richard Wiseman, discovered that lucky people were

lucky because of personal characteristics rather than some mysterious fate. He found that it *was* their character. Through interviews
and tests, Wiseman found among other things that lucky people are
more relaxed, and that they tend to see not only what they are looking for, but also what they are *not* looking for. They are open to the
new and unexpected, while others less lucky (and often more neurotic) are more closed—they look only for what they have in mind,
and often do not find it. The lucky ones are those who multiply their
chances as they notice an article in the newspaper, hear in a conversation a comment that might be useful to them, spot a banknote on
the ground—and do not let a happy opportunity pass. All this happens not by magic, not out of luck, but because they are open and
present and in resonance with the chances life brings. While others,
less fortunate, are closed in their fantasies and obsessed with their
impossible desires, the fortunate ones are simply more attentive.

Attention to the present renders everything more interesting because the world, rather than being an indistinct shadow, takes ever-
newer forms. I first became aware of this fact when, as a child, I met
Aldous Huxley. I have already spoken of him in the introduction,
when I mentioned his remark that to be a little kinder was the best
way to develop our potential. For him, awareness was the foundation for kindness—as well as the opening to an infinitely interesting
world. For Huxley, awareness changes the world around us into a
Gaza, the Babylonian paradise rich in countless treasures and won-
ders. I was nine years old when once we were seated at a table together. I knew that he was interested in everything—he described
himself as "encyclopedically ignorant." So I went out in the garden
and fetched a huge hairy caterpillar, then placed it in front of him—
not as a joke, but as an object of contemplation. Even though one or
two of the company were upset, clearly I had not made a mistake,
for he took from his pocket a magnifying glass he always carried

and studied the caterpillar. "Most extraordinary!" he said—one of his favorite expressions. If we live in the here and now, each moment is a surprise, every instant a new wonder.

But it often fails to work this way. Onto the present we superimpose our expectations and opinions, based on the past or the future. We meet someone, and we already anticipate what she will be like and what she will say. We find ourselves in a situation, and we believe we know what will happen. We live in an impoverished present, robbed of its essential qualities: surprise and novelty. The result is boredom. We are like tourists who visit places they have already seen in the brochures: They see nothing new and find only what they expect to find.

On this theme, Buddha expresses a fundamental concept in one of his discourses: In what you see, let there be only the seeing; in what you hear, let there be only the hearing. It means, Put in brackets your ideas about what you expect to find, and meet the present moment without preconceived notions, with bare attention and in a state of pure openness. You must allow yourself to be surprised by the present moment.

TO BE IN THE PRESENT IS A NECESSARY CONDITION FOR ANY kind of relationship. If I am distracted and not present, where am I? And if I am not here, who is relating in my place? What ghost, what robot have I appointed to represent me? Here is an example: I am at a restaurant with my son Emilio. Now and then, people who know me but do not know him come to this restaurant. Emilio has fairly long hair; he rather likes his blond curls. He has a masculine face, but to a distracted eye, which sees only the curls and thinks in stereotypes, Emilio could look like a girl. We are seated in this restaurant and a group of my acquaintances enters. "Hi, how are you?

And this lovely girl, is she your daughter? *Ciao.*" And off they go. Emilio is angry. He does not like being taken for a girl. Two minutes pass, and in walks another group of people I know. And once again they ask me who is this pretty girl. Then they leave and just miss seeing Emilio cry with rage. A little later still, and my friend and colleague Virgilio arrives and, having noticed us, approaches. Emilio gives me an ominous glance: Is it all going to happen again? But Virgilio is aware. He loves to tend his vegetable garden for a few hours each day; it is his form of meditation. Maybe this is what helps him live in the here and now. Virgilio looks at Emilio, touches him on the shoulder, greets him, and, jokingly calls him *capellone* ("longhair"), including him in the conversation. Emilio smiles. It is so simple: If we are in the present, we truly see the person in front of us—otherwise he or she is just an idea. In fact, being in the present is the only way we can enter into relation with another.

To be in the present with someone else is a gift. The gift of attention is perhaps the most precious and envied of all, even though we do not always realize it. To be there. To be totally available. This is what we secretly hope other people will do for us, and we know it will give us healing relief, space, energy. I remember an extreme example recounted to me by a rather eccentric friend of mine. This friend was having psychotherapy sessions with a therapist who was equally nonconformist. At one point, my friend felt very sleepy, said that she would like to go to sleep, and did so. She woke up the next morning: The therapist not only had made no objection, but had remained awake all night, near to her, present and alert.

This is an extreme, indeed heroic, example. Yet think of all the people who have not given you the attention you needed: husband, wife, children, friends, colleagues, bosses, doctors, teachers, employees. Think of someone who, while you are talking to him, is looking elsewhere, or reading the paper, or mentioning a subject that is irrelevant to what you are saying, or just walks away. Inattention has a disruptive, depressing aspect, which saps our vitality and robs us of our self-confidence. It can arouse all our latent feelings of inferiority and make us feel like nothing. In my work with people, I often hear stories of people who make love with their partner but meanwhile fantasize about making love with somebody else more desirable, or just imagine being somewhere else. To me that is the epitome of absence.

Mindfulness, or attention, on the other hand, has a magical aspect that gives vitality. I am speaking of *pure* attention—without judgement or advice. To pay attention means that we are able to keep at bay the quarrelsome din that continually invades and tries to seduce the mind. In this way, attention becomes a moral quality, like love and justice. We usually think of attention as a neutral process: "Watch your head!" "Be careful crossing the street!" But even here is an implicit ethical dimension, because the failure of attention can endanger the lives of many people, as we have seen in countless tragedies: accidents at the workplace, taking the wrong medicines, people hit by cars because they did not look before crossing, parachutes not properly folded, aircraft that crash. Inattention may be disastrous.

And yet we rarely value it as it deserves. In the school of psychotherapy where I teach, cards with evocative words written on them are pinned to the wall to remind us of certain qualities, "harmony," "serenity," and so on (it is a psychosynthesis technique). Someone once put the card "attention" on a low ceiling beam, to stop people from bumping their heads. Thus from its status as a moral quality, "attention" had been downgraded to the function of street signal. But attention is not merely for preventing accidents. It was a good idea to place the card on the low beam, as long as we do not forget that it also means "being available," "caring," "listening."

To pay attention means to be awake, thus to be aware of what is right in front of us. I notice, for instance, that this person in front of me is pale, is wearing a new dress, is uncomfortable or happy, looks like she hasn't slept well, or looks in good form. Chances are that I am in touch with my feelings for that person, I know how to relate. The same holds for the world around us. Indeed, the ecological tragedies with which our planet is struggling are a result of our inattention. We have not paid enough attention to what is all around us, and to the consequences of what we are doing to it. A plastic bottle thrown in a field, recyclable rubbish merely dumped, or ugly concrete ruining our scenery are results of mindlessness. All we have to do is open our eyes.

Attention is thus a form of kindness, and lack of attention is the greatest form of rudeness. Sometimes it is a form of violence, especially when children are concerned. Negligence is justifiably regarded as abuse when it reaches an unacceptable level, but in small doses it is one of the most common childhood ignominies. In someone else's presence we can hang up the sign "Back soon" and keep thinking our own thoughts. Inside our heads are thousands of possible trains of thought, seductive and terrifying, all clamoring for our attention. We can listen to them, lose ourselves in them, and the person in front of us might not even notice. But we can also pay attention. Inattention is cold and hard. Attention is warm and caring. It makes our best possibilities flower.

An African story tells of a king whose wife is always sad and weak. One day he notices that a poor fisherman living near the kingdom has a wife who is the picture of health and happiness. So he asks the fisherman, "How do you manage to make her so happy?" "It is easy," replies the fisherman. "I feed her meat of the tongue." The king thinks he now has the solution. He orders the best butchers in the kingdom to provide meat of the tongue for his wife, whom he now

places on an enriched diet. But his hopes are spurned. She deterio-
rates. The king is angry, goes to the fisherman, and says, "Let us exchange wives. I want a more cheerful one." The fisherman is forced
to accept this proposition, though he does it sorrowfully. Time
passes, and bit by bit the new wife of the king, to his dismay, becomes sick and pale, while his ex-wife, living with the fisherman,
now glows with health and joy. One day at the market, she meets the
king, who hardly recognizes her. He is amazed: "Come back to me!"
"Never!" Then she explains, "Every day, my new husband, when he
comes home, sits with me, tells me stories, listens to me, sings, makes
me laugh, enlivens me. That is the 'meat of the tongue': someone
who talks to me and pays attention to me. All day long I look forward to the evening." Then the king understands and feels both immense remorse and the great energy of a true turning point. Will he
be able to make up for his past mistakes? Can he now be truly awake?

Attention is the medium through which kindness can flow. No
attention, no kindness. And also, no warmth, no intimacy, no relationship. Think of your best moments with others: I am sure you
were right there, fully attentive. By paying attention, we attribute
meaning and importance, we offer nourishment, and we are close to
another human being. We give the presence and the energy of the
heart. We can care for, we can love, and we can enjoy one another
only in the present. And if conflict arises, we deal best with it not by
daydreaming, but by being awake. For all our relationships, the only
time is now.

EMPATHY

Expansion of Consciousness

Although I am not a musician, I once had the opportunity to hold in my hands an exquisitely made violin dating to the eighteenth century. What amazed me, even more than its harmonious lines or the beautiful grain of its wood, was that, holding it, I could feel it vibrate. It was not an inert object. It resonated with the various sounds that happened to resonate around it: another violin, a tram passing in the street, a human voice. If you hold an ordinary, factory-made violin, that just does not happen. There can be hundreds of sounds around it, and the violin remains numb. In order to obtain the fine sensitivity and extraordinary resonance of the old violin, the makers had to have an exceptional knowledge of wood and its seasoning; they were supported by the artisan tradition of generations, and they were endowed with the talent of cutting the wood and furnishing the instrument.

This marvelous responsiveness is an active virtue. It is the capacity of the violin to enter into resonance, and it goes hand in hand with its capacity to create sound of extraordinary quality—music with a soul, able to move and to inspire.

We humans are, or at least can be, like that violin. Since birth we have been able to resonate with other human beings. A newborn cries when in the presence of other crying babies. Bit by bit, empathy—which at first is only a simple instinctual capacity to resonate—develops and becomes the capacity to understand other people's feelings and points of view, to identify with them.

But if this capacity does not develop sufficiently or if it is thwarted, we are in trouble. If we are insensitive to the emotions of others, each relationship becomes an impossible charade. And if we see others not as living subjects but as things, on par with a refrigerator or a street lamp, we allow ourselves to manipulate and even to violate them. When instead empathy is fully developed, our existence is immeasurably richer and more varied. We are able to step out of our selves and enter into the lives of others. Relationships then become a source of interest, of emotional and spiritual nourishment.

However varied and vast our inner world may be, it is still a closed system, ultimately narrow and oppressive. Our thoughts, worries, desires: Is that all there is? Sometimes it seems so. But to step out of this world and enter other ones—the passions, fears, hopes, and suffering of other human beings—is akin to an interplanetary voyage. Yet it is a feat far simpler to accomplish. Closing ourselves to other people makes us imbalanced, whereas participating in their lives helps us to be healthier and happier. Self-attention or self-focus is correlated with greater depression and anxiety. We know this much for sure: People who are most concerned with themselves and less with others are more likely to feel fearful or unhappy.

Empathy has been necessary to our survival since prehistoric times: Human beings can thrive only in community. And that is impossible if they cannot read the emotions and intentions of others. In small, everyday matters, too, the same principle holds: A person who tries to jump the line, or drops rubbish in the street, or makes a noise when others are trying to sleep is doing so because he is incapable of conceiving others' reactions. Empathy is a prerequisite for communication, collaboration, and social cohesion. If we annul it, we return to savagery—or cease to exist.

Empathy is the best means of improving any relationship. Have you ever witnessed a quarrel in which neither party had the least intention or ability to see things from the other's point of view? How painful. Yet it happens, and we see it day after day in the arena of international relations. Empathy is what is missing most, and what would most help resolve age-old, dangerous racial problems and prejudices. That is why it is so important at this time.

Because of the growing mobility of an ever greater number of people, we increasingly find ourselves face to face with individuals belonging to other cultures. They have grown up in environments totally different from ours. They have a different religion, a different physical appearance. Their customs, food, clothes, attitudes to sexuality, to time, to manners and sense of duty, to work and money— just about everything—is different. Our first reaction is often suspicion. It has been shown that racial prejudice has deep roots, and that suspicion is not rational but rather based on an immediate emotional reaction that is beyond our control. Thus even those who in theory say they have no prejudices, really do have them.

Training in empathy is perhaps one of the most urgent needs in our educational programs at all levels. Yehudi Menuhin, the great violinist, once made an extraordinary statement in an interview: If

German youth had been brought up not only to appreciate the music of Beethoven, but to sing and dance traditional Jewish music, the Holocaust would not have happened.

But empathy does not only resolve problems; it helps us feel better. Studies have shown that people who are more capable of empathy are also more satisfied in life, healthier, less dogmatic, and more creative. Despite all these advantages, empathy evokes a good deal of resistance. The willingness to identify with another for the sake of understanding him is seen by some as a weakness. Yet it is the best solution for everyone. The moment someone feels understood and realizes that we see the validity in his point of view and the legitimacy of his demands, he changes. In this way we can avoid countless complications.

Some time ago while driving, I abruptly stopped the car to let a child, who had suddenly run out, cross the street. The driver behind me bumped into my car. As we got out of the cars and approached one another, I saw he was on the warpath. Even though he had not uttered a single word, I could feel he was in emergency mode. Yet there was no damage to either car. So I spoke first. I could have said, "I am right." It was true but useless, if not harmful. Instead I said, "I was going quite fast and stopped suddenly. You did not expect that. Sorry. Are you okay?" Immediately, the man changed. Every line on his face moved imperceptibly. In a fraction of a second, his defenses dropped. Yes, he was okay. I saw surprise in his eyes: His opponent was interested in how he felt. Then I saw relief: No need to fight. Finally, he simply shook my hand and left. What could have become an argument full of rage and fury was resolved in a few seconds.

So empathy is a means at our disposal for bringing relief and contentment to another person. It is no coincidence that, according to many psychotherapists, empathy is the essential ingredient of the successful therapeutic relationship. Suffering individuals do not need diagnoses, advice, interpretations, manipulations. They need genuine and total empathy. When at last they feel that someone identifies with their experience, in that moment they are able to let go of their suffering and are healed.

Something similar happens in the medical field. It has been shown that the more empathic a doctor is, the more her patients see her as competent. Unfortunately, it has also been shown that medical students have greater capacity for empathy at the start of their internship than at the end. Shouldn't we expect a bit more of the training for a helping profession?

However, we can also have too much of a good thing. We can easily overdose on empathy. We hear about other people's troubles and suffering, we identify with them completly, and we end up exhausted and torn, perhaps even enraged. We can lose our center.

Toward the end of her life, my mother, still in good health, would sometimes have a mental lapse. One day she told me that while driving, she would at times place herself so much in other people's shoes that when the light turned red for her, she would think, "It's green for them," and would, placing herself in their shoes, go through the red light. She would realize what she had done only after having driven through several red lights and seen the outraged reactions of other drivers. Oblivious empathy is a danger. We first need to be sure we are in touch with ourselves and our own needs, in possession of our own space and time. We must have our own life under control before we try to solve other people's problems. Otherwise we are in for an accident.

Empathy is an ingredient of the emotional intelligence necessary for acting competently and efficiently in today's world. Greater empathy means doing better at school, finding a job, having satisfying relationships, and communicating with your children. Think of an advertising agent incapable of imagining people's reactions, a musician with no relationship to his audience, a teacher who cannot understand his students, or a parent who doesn't know what his children are going through. How are they going to cope?

A revealing aspect of empathy, a true test, is joy at other people's success—a virtue that Buddhists call *mudita*. Let's say a friend of yours suddenly becomes successful, or his son shows talents of which your children do not even dream, or has a new, intensely beautiful relationship, such as you perhaps have secretly desired yourself. What is your response? Are you happy for him? Or do you feel a secret displeasure that the same has not happened to you? Do you make comparisons, or wonder why you haven't been so lucky, or feel envious? Empathic joy for the success of another is rare, except perhaps for our own children, who we feel are extensions of us. It is not easy to feel unconditional joy for the happiness given to someone else and denied to us. If we can, it means we have come a long way.

But empathy is not a cheerful, carefree quality. On the contrary, it has more to do with failure than success, with suffering than with joy. It is exactly when things are going badly that empathy is beneficial. True, we are glad when someone shares our happy moments. But it is when we are in distress that we need someone to understand us.

For empathy to be full and genuine, the person feeling it must have a healthy relationship with his own and others' suffering. Pain is by definition what we most abhor. We run away from it when we can. Avoiding pain is really the basis of health, and reducing it to a minimum is a sign of wisdom. But a certain amount of pain is inevitable in our life. We are all fragile. Sooner or later we all are sick, make mistakes, fail, are disappointed in what life brings, or lose a person we love. We all suffer. And we have to come to terms with our suffering.

How do you face pain? It is not easy. Some pretend not to feel it, smiling the whole way through: "It's nothing." Some are proud of it: "My headache is worse than yours." Some like to show it off, describing all their woes in detail: "Let me tell you the history of my cavities." Some blame God or destiny, believing themselves to be the target of divine wrath or of adversity: "It always happens to me!" And some are always complaining, even when the pain is over, not only about real pain but also about possible pain, as though not wanting to be taken by surprise. Some fight the whole time, whether there is cause to or not. And finally, some simply become discouraged and depressed, and withdraw from life: "I give up."

These are all ineffective ways of dealing with suffering. They can perhaps give some illusory comfort, but mostly they just perpetuate or increase suffering instead of eliminating it. The best way to face pain is directly, with sincerity and courage. To enter into it, as into a tunnel, then to come out the other side.

The myth of Chiron has much to teach us about this attitude. Chiron is born of a rape: His father, Cronos, the chief of the gods, had changed himself into a horse to chase a woman, then caught her and raped her. The son thus born is monstrous—half-horse, half-man—and is straightaway rejected by his mother. So Chiron is born in ignominy and suffering. At first he copes by denying the terrible truth. With the help of Apollo, he cultivates everything that is noble and intelligent—the human side. He becomes an expert in the arts of medicine, herbs, astrology, archery. His fame spreads so that kings want him as teacher for their sons and daughters. But one day Chiron is accidentally wounded in the knee by a poisoned arrow. Were he merely a man, he would die, but he is son of a god, therefore he cannot die. He can only suffer.

He suffers unspeakably: His mobility is compromised, and he becomes dependent on his daughter. The arrow has struck him in the lower part of the body, the animal part, of which he is ashamed, and which he tries his best to forget since it reminds him of his painful rejection. In such a state, Chiron cannot be a teacher of kings, but can only help the poor and the suffering. He carries out this task with extraordinary skill. Try as he may to relieve his own suffering, he fails. But with his knowledge, sensitivity, and his capacity for empathy acquired through pain, he succeeds in healing the suffering of others. He has become the wounded healer.

At one point, Chiron learns that his pain will end if he renounces immortality. He must give up the last of his privileges. He decides to do so, and descends for nine days to the Underworld. Finally, Zeus raises him to the heavens, turning him into the constellation of the Centaur, or Sagittarius, we can still see on clear summer nights. At last, he finds the peace and union with the cosmos he had always sought.

Chiron is not a macho hero like Achilles or Hercules. He is an antihero. He wins because of, not in spite of, his fragility. He becomes empathic and heals others, only when he no longer tries at all costs to affirm his intelligence and talent. He attains supreme realization, union with the All, only when, instead of fighting pain, he accepts it.

If I deny my suffering, it is hard for me to identify with the pain of others. If I boast about it, I will see others as competitors and will not likely be sensitive to their problems. My own suffering is the grounds for empathy.

Naturally, our empathy is greatest toward those whose suffering is similar to ours. Someone mistreated as a child will be able to understand another with the same kind of trauma. The victim of a car accident, or of sexual abuse, or someone who has been bankrupt, or who has lost a child, can better understand others in similar tragedies. And can better help them. Not surprisingly, the area of trauma becomes the area of service.

This is the hardest and most painful way to develop empathy. It is a way I do not wish on anyone, yet somehow it is everyone's destiny. Pain is, in varying doses, a companion for life. But not all its effects are tragic. When confronted honestly, pain can bear fruits of great importance. It digs deep inside us, opens us, sometimes violently, makes us grow more mature, discover emotions and resources we were not aware of, develops our sensitivity—and perhaps our humility and wisdom. It is a harsh reminder of what is essential. It can connect us to others. Yes, suffering can harden us or make us more cynical, but it can also make us kinder.

Luckily, there are other ways besides pain for developing empathy. Knowledge and practice of the arts—literature, painting, and above all dance—apparently include among their benefits the increased capacity for empathy. But the easiest and most direct method consists in putting yourself, with your imagination, in the other person's place. The first to adopt this technique was Laura Huxley in her book *You Are Not the Target*. Here is how she does it: After we have had a difficulty with someone important in our life, such as an argument with our husband or wife, we relive the episode, identifying with the other. If we succeed, we can see the world, including ourselves, from a fresh, often surprising, viewpoint. I have seen people who practiced this exercise make extraordinary realizations. They saw they never before had truly known someone close to them.

Once I happened to be in Laura Huxley's studio, and a wonderful piece of music was playing, one of Mozart's piano concertos. In the next room, Laura was making phone calls to help a young Thai woman who had recently arrived in the United States, and who was pregnant. I could hear Laura speaking on the phone, and though I could not make out her words, I knew what she was talking about. I heard in her voice the worry for this girl, the desire to help her. Usually I prefer to listen to music without other sounds. But this time Laura's words from the next room blended magically with Mozart's music. I could feel that Laura had put herself in the shoes of the Thai girl, could understand how displaced she was, how alone, how desperate in a foreign country, and, as if that were not enough, pregnant. Laura's voice became part of Mozart's music; it was as if the music were helping me find the beauty of solidarity, and the voice seeking help were helping me understand the wondrous richness of Mozart's music. In that moment, I understood the meaning of compassion: participating in the suffering of other human beings with sincere and intense identification.

Children can often feel immediate and intense compassion, perhaps more so than adults. We grown-ups have already been through much and have a tougher skin. When we pass a poor drunk sleeping on the street or a woman begging, perhaps we do not even notice. But children are not protected from the evils and suffering of the world. I remember when my son Jonathan was four or five and saw, for the first time, a homeless man: a wreck of a human being, as you can often see in the big cities. For us it is normal, we are used to it. Not so for a child. Jonathan looked at that man, who was dressed in rags, hair long and matted, bitterness in his face, murmuring nonsense and rummaging among garbage. Jonathan's face showed astonishment at first, then an expression of infinite pity, mixed with outrage: How could such indignity exist?

Another time, Jonathan saw a decrepit old lady, bent and unwell, going up some stairs, each step costing her enormous effort. Right then, Jonathan realized that in life there is the suffering of old age. I don't know what he was thinking at the time, but I knew that his heart ached, that he was feeling compassion. Sometimes it takes a child to rediscover our own feelings.

Compassion is the final and noblest result of empathy. It is a spiritual quality because it brings us out of selfishness and greed. It includes everyone, even the least able, least pleasant, least intelligent. It opens and unites us to others. It fills our heart.

But you could define compassion another way: As relation in its pure state. Often in our relationships, judgment reigns. We like to judge, it makes us feel superior. Or perhaps there is an old debt, or a wish for vendetta (a dish we savor, but cannot digest). Maybe competitiveness gets in the way, or the need to give advice, or the lust for comparisons. Or perhaps we see the other as a means to achieve some end. All these are interferences that harm and distort the relationship.

Now let us imagine a relationship, any relationship, in its pure state. Let us imagine it is stripped of judgment, spite, comparison, and so on. We find ourselves in front of the other without screen or defense. Then we are immediately able to resonate. Freed of the ballast, we feel lighter. We forget our hurry. We are free. Then empathy is possible. And so too is knowledge. If you and I are open to each other, without barriers between us, then I feel your feelings and you feel mine. I feel understood by you and you by me. If you are suffering, I want your suffering to end, and if I am suffering, I know you will support me. If you are happy, I am too, and if things are going well for me, I know you are pleased.

And maybe nothing more is needed.

HUMILITY

You Are Not the Only One Around

One piece of advice we can receive is "Know your own strength."

Think of a person who faces the world without knowing his capabilities and limitations—someone with misguided notions about himself, who dreams of being powerful, rich, and admired for a host of talents he does not have. Such a person is incapable of self-judgment. Equipped with mistaken ideas, he enters the great arena of the world ready to compete and excel. You can only shudder at the thought of his fate. He is like a child who thinks he can walk miles, but who tires after only two hundred feet.

To know your own weaknesses and to accept them, even if it is painful. To be honest. To chase illusions away and realize how much you do not know. To treasure life's lessons. That is humility. And humility is a great strength.

The Last Emperor, a film by Bernardo Bertolucci, tells the true story of the Chinese emperor who was brought up as a god in a magnificent abode, served and honored as the center of the universe. He was isolated from the world, solitary and unaware, in his grand palace. But great social upheavals in Chinese society put an end to this privilege. At the story's turning point, when the emperor has to flee, he is forced to realize he is not divine but human; not superior to others but equal. The extraordinary structure that had isolated him from the world, that had made him believe he was God, that had cradled him in his unreality, crumbles. The emperor discovers that he is a man like others, subject to pain and uncertainty. By humbling himself in this way, he discovers who he is. And this realization, painful as it may be, is not a defeat, but an unexpected victory.

When you know your own limits, you are ready to begin again. A Zen saying tells that in the mind of the beginner exist infinite possibilities, in the mind of the expert only a few. Much better to be a beginner, even in our field of presumed expertise. To be sure, when we are experts we make a fine impression, we risk less, we defend ourselves with our reputation, and we feel secure. But we learn little, because we think we already know. Instead, as beginners, we are always willing to learn, and to ask innocent, even stupid, questions.

A recent study has shown that, if you want to be at your best in learning, humility is your tool. The humblest students, who think they know the least, do more tests and research when given a problem, and prove to be more efficient than those who think they already have the answer. It is hardly surprising. A student who overestimates her own knowledge will fail the exam, just as a sportswoman who underestimates her competitors will lose. Being humble means you work harder and prepare yourself better.

So humility is linked to learning and to renewing ourselves. We often reach a point in our lives where, rather than remaining open to learning, we want safe and predictable plans. And we prefer the prestige of teacher to the humility of student. So we shut the door to reality; we take everything for granted and give up questioning, give up admitting that what we know is possibly no longer true, that our cultural equipment is beginning to be obsolete. For love of comfort, we renounce the labor of skepticism and research. In the extreme case, we become zombies. And what a pity, when things could be different. One of Goya's etchings shows a decrepit old man, and underneath we read the two words *Aun aprendo*, "I am still learning." That is intellectual vitality at its best. That is humility.

A similar tendency happens in relationship with others. We can exclude a priori the possibility that others can teach us anything new. Or else we have the choice to recognize that all around us are people who, with their experiences, feelings, and ideas, their dreams and ideals, can enrich our lives—we need only look and listen. We need the courage to ask ourselves: What can I learn from this person? *Aun aprendo . . .*

Thus humility is at times hard, even painful. It is always beneficial, however. The gift of humility greets us in our most difficult moments. We often become humbler after a failure. We understand we were not as clever or as strong as we thought. We realize our humanness: We are fallible and vulnerable. If we manage not to be overwhelmed by our defeats, big and small, they will show us what we can and cannot do. If only successes come our way, we are in trouble. We have lost our yardstick.

When we are aware of our strengths and weaknesses, we are less likely to flaunt how clever we are. On the other hand, many insecure people look like an advertising agency for themselves. They are busy trying to prove how good they are. Not content to be what they are, they must be better than others, and that becomes their purpose in life. Because they are busy competing, they have less energy for what really counts: for learning and for creating, for rapport with others, for being open to a world full of interesting opportunities.

A host of research shows that the more competitive we are, the less efficient and receptive to learning we will be, and also the less creative, because the anxiety of competition distracts us from the task at hand. Humility is just the opposite. A humble person does not need to triumph in order to justify his existence. He knows well that some others are better than he is, and accepts it. This elementary fact has huge consequences. If I do not try to be what I am not, I give myself permission to be what I am.

ONE DAY, THE OFFICIALS OF THE CHINESE EMPEROR (ANOTHER emperor, an earlier time) went looking for Chuang Tzu, the Taoist philosopher who lived as a poor man, but alone and free. The emperor had heard that Chuang Tzu was very wise and wanted to install him as counselor at his court. He would have offered him any honor, wealth, or privilege. Chuang Tzu replied, "Think of a turtle. What do you think it prefers? To be alive and rolling in the mud, or dead, its shell gilded and polished to serve as a jewel box?" "Better to be alive," answered the officials. "Well then, leave me to roll in the mud."

Chuang Tzu rejected the heavy chains of a role. The word "role" comes from the Latin *rotulus*, the scroll of paper on which an actor's lines would be written in ancient times. Roles are all that is predefined and predictable in us. When they are important, roles help us hide our weaknesses and give us a fictitious strength. If I am president, I am no longer the dyspeptic who cannot get along with his wife. If I am professor, I can forget for a while about my depression and backache. I can impress my students and be important.

I had a chance to see the tricky bondage of roles—as well as freedom from them—early in my career. My teacher, Roberto Assagioli, was becoming well known overseas, and a stream of visitors arrived to meet him. Among them came a group of VIPs in the field of psychotherapy and spirituality. Assagioli would meet them in the afternoon, I would take them during the morning in a series of group sessions. I, the novice, had to guide these noteworthy people in a series of psychosynthesis exercises. How were they going to respond? Would they see my weak points, would they tolerate me patiently, or would they embarrass me with some tough question or malicious remark? I was anxious. The group went well: no blunders, no disasters as I feared. Nonetheless, I noticed how all participants, however gracious and witty, identified with their own roles. They all asked the questions and made the statements that were expected of their public role. Only one person in the group was different from all the others: Virginia Satir, the famous American family therapist. She behaved like a beginner. She did the exercises and spoke of her spontaneous reactions and thoughts, completely forgetful of her standing and professional expertise. I still remember the relief and gratitude I felt in the presence of this woman, renowned in her field, but willing to put aside her public image and start from scratch.

I am indeed suspicious of the word "image" as it is sometimes used. Politicians, actors, even common mortals cultivate their "image." This procedure presumes a difference between their public image and what they really are. Outwardly you see the image, knowingly cultivated by the experts: Here I am, smiling, athletic, well dressed, and successful. But what lies behind the image? I want to know: What is the *substance*? There, in the dark, is a small, frightened person who wants to be loved and admired but dreads solitude and failure.

Where image and substance coincide, we have humility. Then we no longer try to appear different from what we are, but are at ease with all our faults and weaknesses. What sort of person do you like to deal with? And what sort—proud or humble—do you think is likely to be kind, and to be good company as well? I have no doubt that someone who tries to show how clever she is cannot be truly kind. Her kindness will be condescending. Only a humble person can be kind, because, not playing any one-upmanship game, she is able to enjoy a relationship in which no one triumphs, and therefore all win.

In an Afghan story, a king governs his country in a dictatorial and ruthless way. He commands his subjects and harasses them with unjust taxes, not caring for them—in his eyes they all are mere pawns without faces. One day, he goes hunting and chases a gazelle. The gazelle runs fast, leading the king into unknown places, on and on till he is lost, right to the edge of the desert. Now he sees the gazelle, now he doesn't, then he sees it again just for a moment in the distance, finally he loses sight of it altogether.

The king, disappointed, decides to go back, but because he has strayed so far, he is no longer sure of the way. A terrible dust storm blows for three days. The king is surrounded by thrashing dust. He wanders without knowing where he is going. By the end of the storm, he is alone in the desert. He is lost. His clothes are torn to shreds, his face unrecognizable, distorted by fear and fatigue. He meets some nomads. When he tells them he is the king, they laugh, yet they help him, give him food, and tell him the way. With great effort the king returns to his palace, but the guards—his own guards—do not recognize him and do not let him in. They take him to be a poor crazed fool. From behind the gates, the king sees the substitute king: a mysterious spirit who has taken his place and is pretending to be him, reigning like he did—arrogant and mean-spirited.

Bit by bit the king learns to live in poverty. He manages, but never without the help of others. One day someone offers him water to drink, another day someone else gives him food, or shelter, or work.

And he, too, puts in effort. He helps whomever he can. Once he saves the life of a child trapped inside a house on fire. Another time he offers food to someone hungrier than he is. Slowly the king comes to understand that his subjects are people like him, and that in life, people must care for each other. He learns that life is more beautiful and interesting when we love and help one another. In the end, he realizes that the reigning king is an illusion created by the Angel of Humility. The time has come for him to return to his palace and reign again. But this time the king governs wisely and kindly because he has learned the priceless lesson of humility.

The story of the king teaches an essential element of humility: I am not the only one—other people exist. Anyone would agree with this truism, but how many actually live according to it? From childhood we carry undeclared beliefs that if stated explicitly seem absurd. Nevertheless they are active, like an old program that has never been deactivated. Our implicit and irrational belief that we are different and special is a remnant of childhood and makes us behave as if we were not subject to common laws and rules.

Humility is the death of this secret conviction. It is a Copernican revolution; we see that we are not the center of the universe. To realize we are not as important as we thought can be painful, but it is also liberating. The American president Theodore Roosevelt used to go outside at night to look at the stars and remind himself of the vastness of the universe. To be head of a great nation had a completely different feeling in the context of the galaxies.

Here we have an essential condition for kindness. How can we be kind if, deep down, we think we are special and not subject to the laws others have to obey? We have all seen parked cars taking up two spaces, where a parking spot is as valuable as a car's weight in gold; or passengers on crowded trains, their legs stretched out onto the opposite seat, pretending to be asleep while others ride standing up;

or people smoking where nobody wants to inhale their smoke. If you ask these people, "Do others exist?" they will look at you bewildered and reply yes. But perhaps they have not realized the vast and inconvenient implications of this simple fact.

To accept that we are on the same level as everybody else, precarious, perhaps banal, that we need others, and that we are imperfect in an imperfect world, can be unpleasant. So we defend ourselves from this realization with a multitude of fantasies and hopes. Yet it is precisely by understanding and accepting our weaknesses that we become fully human: This is our reality, this is how we truly are. It is a solid base on which we can make contact with other people. All those who feel this way are humble. You feel good when you are with them, because they possess that strange mixture of serenity and irony that only humility can offer. Isn't that the best way to be kind?

Humility is also inherent in the capacity to make do—a precious attitude in times such as ours when waste is the very basis of economic development, greed a lifestyle, and demand for new privileges a social duty. Those who make do with what they have are often considered losers. Yet they are the ones most likely to be serene and happy.

I remember an evening at a Chinese restaurant when our friends, after the meal, took out their Christmas presents for our kids— good, thoughtful presents, among them a compact camera with a roll of film. Suddenly I noticed a little Chinese girl watching us. She was a member of the family who ran the restaurant. I could not work out what she was thinking, but I felt a little ill at ease; perhaps she was wishing for such gifts too. I was soon distracted by the conversation at the table, and shortly afterward we left the restaurant. While waiting outside for one of our group to fetch the car, I noticed through the window that the girl had gone to our table and was playing delightedly with the empty film container, a simple plastic cylinder. Then she looked up at us and, catching our gaze, smiled.

That was a lesson in humility. In the Age of Hurry, when we often do not even have the time to savor what life gives us yet seek ever new products and stimuli, when nothing seems enough, to see someone happy with almost nothing is a huge relief and an example to remember.

To sum up: Humility places us in a state where learning becomes possible. It gives us a taste for simplicity; and when we are simpler, we are also more genuine. Humility put into practice allows us to touch reality as it is. No more dreams, fantasies, or illusions. I am one among many, mortal and limited, a human being among human beings. I do not have to prove myself superior to anyone. Others exist, each with their needs, their realities, their hopes, and their dramas, and I am one among billions of people who exist on this planet, which is, itself, no more than a speck of dust in sidereal space. My life is no more than a moment in vast universal time.

Realizing and accepting this fact makes us different—humbler, capable of benevolent irony, better able to stay in our place and make room for others. Humility helps us find our place under the stars.

PATIENCE

Have You Left Your Soul Behind?

In Ethiopia, a man and a woman, both widowed and still young, meet and fall in love. They decide to start a new family together. However, a problem comes up: the man has a little boy who is still full of sorrow over his mother's death. The child is hostile toward the new wife and rejects her as a mother. She prepares special dishes for him, sews him lovely clothes, tries always to be kind. But he does not even speak to her, and thus completely shuts her out.

She goes to the sorcerer: "What can I do to be accepted as mother?" The sorcerer is very clever—he finds the answer to every problem, and everyone has faith in him. "Come back to me with three lion's whiskers," he tells her. The woman is incredulous. How can anyone take three whiskers from a lion without being devoured? "Come back with three lion's whiskers!"

The woman looks for a lion. It takes a long time, but at last she finds one. She keeps her distance—it looks so frightening. For a long time, she just watches it from afar. It comes and goes. She waits and waits. Then the woman decides to offer it food. Getting a bit closer, she leaves some meat and goes away. Every day she does the same. Gradually the lion gets used to her, till finally the woman is part of its life. The lion is calm with the woman—by now it knows it can expect only good things from her—and she is less afraid. One day, when the lion is asleep, she removes the three whiskers. Easy.

The woman does not need to return to the sorcerer. Now she understands. During these months, she has changed. She has understood the value of patience. With the child she does the same as with the lion. She waits faithfully and approaches him little by little, respecting his tempo and his territory, without invading him but without giving up on him, either. In the end, the child accepts her as his mother. This woman has won the child's heart with her patience.

The virtue of patience is first of all about dealing with difficult people: Those who won't listen to reason, easily get upset, and just refuse to get along. Like the child in the story, their own deep wounds prevent them from relating to others with even a minimum of openness and sanity.

Then we also have those people who clearly make a nuisance of themselves. Let's face it, in our everyday life we are destined to run into them all the time: the ones who interrupt us every other word, who criticize us for the sake of criticizing, who insist on getting our time or attention or money, who whine or sabotage, who start talking to us and won't let us go even though they know we are in a hurry, and so on. Everything is relative, so we are all at different times both victims and, to some extent, persecutors. We have all met difficult people, and have all somehow been difficult ourselves for others—perhaps without even realizing it.

But some people are champions. They get first prize for pushing our buttons. Our reaction when faced with them is to feel irritated. And we either express our annoyance or suffer in silence. It is also possible, however, to practice the art of patience and help these people feel better about themselves.

I had proof of this once on an airplane. To start with, a plane is, for many of us, an extremely frustrating place. It is hard to endure the time, crammed with others for hours in a noisy, unstable contraption. But what happens if our neighbors are a nuisance? Well, behind me on this flight was seated a man who was clearly drunk—and growing louder and more aggressive the more he drank. At one point, he dropped his meal tray: French fries, mushrooms, and macaroni went rolling down the aisle. Then suddenly I was shocked to realize he had brought a huge toad in a box. (Don't ask me how he got past the security check.) Soon the stewardesses stepped in. But instead of reproaching him, as I secretly hoped they would, they began to talk with him, joke, pour him a little more wine, admire the toad; and they cleaned the mess without a word. The drunk calmed down and soon fell asleep.

This is one of the hardest criteria for testing our patience: having to deal with someone insufferable. Those stewardesses get full marks. It seems to me that what works is not to react to the annoyance, but instead to treat the person with skill and kindness. Difficult people are not used to that type of treatment—they are usually neither liked nor tolerated. And what happens if you continually meet with irritation? They end up falling into their role of nuisance. With our own reactions, we all unwittingly help reinforce their role. They are often unhappy people who—believe it or not—awkwardly and desperately try to be accepted.

Patience is also the skill of understanding and respecting your own rhythms and those of others. We have all been victims of impatience: the pressure of deadlines, the aggressive driver on the freeway who suddenly appears in our rearview mirror flashing his headlights, the bus passenger who pushes past everyone to get off first, even when it is clear we are all getting off. All these situations cause us discomfort. When someone imposes on us a rhythm that is not ours, we feel violated.

We have all been on the other side of the fence as well. We have to make an urgent call, while the man inside the telephone booth nonchalantly continues to chatter. Famished, we sit for ages in a restaurant waiting to be noticed by a sour waiter. At the post office, a talkative woman asks a lot of pointless questions, wasting everyone's time.

I am convinced that if we practice patience, we come to understand profound aspects of other people's lives. We understand their rhythms and their weaknesses, thereby knowing their nature intimately. Also, patience is the virtue of all good teachers, who know how to wait for the pupil slowly to mature, instead of pushing him before he is ready. If we rush, we may lose ourselves. But we are so used to hurrying that we do not notice the loss.

A group of scientists had to carry out research in a faraway, almost inaccessible place. A group of Mexican carriers were transporting their equipment by hand. Along the way, all the carriers inexplicably stopped at once. The scientists were astonished, then became irritated, finally furious. Why did they not go on? They were wasting time. The Mexicans seemed to be waiting. Then all at once, they started moving again. One of them explained to the scientists what had happened: "Because we had been going so fast, we had left our souls behind. We stopped to wait for our souls."

We too often leave our souls behind. Caught up in urgency, we forget what is truly important in life. Pushed on by the demon of haste, we forget our souls—our dreams, our warmth, our wonder.

From this viewpoint, it is clear how patience is part of kindness, for how can we be kind if we do not respect the rhythm of others? We forget the soul—theirs and ours. The next time you surprise yourself while hurrying your child, or pacing up and down waiting for a late train, or forgetting to breathe in your haste, ask yourself where you left your soul.

Kindness has a slow pace. Speed has its advantages, to be sure. We can be more efficient, and have a sense of power and control. Not only that, speed stimulates the adrenalin and acts like a drug. Once we have tasted the thrill of it, slowing down becomes boring, even humiliating. If you can go from A to B by plane, why travel by boat?

Yet the Buddhist scholar Lama Govinda told me once that he preferred to travel by ship, bit by bit. This old sage confided to me that for him and for his wife, air travel felt unreal. You are taken too abruptly from one place to another, from one culture and atmosphere to another. Below you, passing by very quickly, are rivers, seas, mountains, cities, countries, and peoples—and you are hardly even aware of this abundance. Traveling more slowly on land or sea, you can more easily comprehend and assimilate the change. Lama Govinda had taken five months to get from his home at the foot of the Himalayas to the Tuscan hills. In later years, when I have been wildly tossed about in a powerful aircraft, or when I arrive too fast in a faraway place that feels alien, I have often thought of Lama Govinda. We cannot all follow his example, but it reminds us of another way of being.

IN ORDER TO BE KIND, WE MUST MAKE TIME. MARTIN BUBER spoke of the difference between the I–Thou and the I–it relationship. An I–it relation transforms the other into a thing, whereas I–Thou is the true relation, the union between two souls. I–it relationships are alienating—they make us what we are not. We then feel lonely and depressed, distant from others. I–Thou is the true encounter, the very substance of our life. According to Buber, in order for this relationship to be possible, there must be no expectation or desire, otherwise we fall into I–it relationship, that is, we transform the other into a means of satisfying our demands. In the rare moments of I–Thou relationship, there is no more urgency to make something happen, no pressure to manipulate or persuade. If urgency arises, the relationship straightaway becomes I–it. If we slow down, we are more likely to meet truly and to know each other.

I am convinced that global cooling goes hand in hand with the accelerated pace in all sectors of modern life. We are under pressure—we cannot afford to waste even a second. Children are made to grow up fast, and we feel proud when they can complete next year's curriculum early. Computers are faster and more powerful. Purchases are instantaneous—we can have almost immediately what we want. Employees have to be able to answer for every minute of their time. Cars are made to go faster, and speed limits are raised. To increase profits, new versions of consumer items come out ever more frequently. "Pointless" activities, like having a chat, meeting in the square or in a park, idling away the time with others, are often discouraged. If all this is happening, inevitably the room for warmth becomes less and less.

One expert on the pace of life, Robert Levine, has been studying time as it is experienced in various cultures. Levine measures three different variables: The time it takes to buy a stamp in a post office, the speed at which pedestrians walk on the street, and the accuracy of clocks in banks. Thus he has discovered that there are speedier cultures, in which punctuality and precision are rewarded, while other cultures are slower and less precise. Western society and Japan are the fastest; Brazil, Indonesia, and Mexico are the slowest. Naturally Levine's study does not claim that one way of perceiving time is better than the other. Cultures are just the way they are. However, from this study, one disadvantage of accelerated living does seem to emerge. In cultures where the pace is hurried, cardiovascular disease is more widespread (with the exception of Japan, where social support and cohesion make up for time pressure). This finding coincides with the many studies on Type A personality. According to that research, the Type A personality—impatient, competitive, and irritable—runs the same risks.

Levine did not find a relationship between pace of life and willingness to help—different factors were at play. But other research has discovered that the more we hurry, the less we are willing to help. My favorite is a study on a group of theology students who had to listen to a lecture on charity, and who then had to move, one by one, to a nearby building. On the way, they met an accomplice of the experimenters. This person was down on the floor, pretending to have fallen and hurt himself. Most of the priests helped him. But when they were pressured and had to hurry from one building to another, the Good Samaritans among them diminished drastically. One of the priests, in his hurry, even stepped over the unfortunate crying actor and headed straight for his destination. We are kinder when we have more time.

In these times of accelerated pace and immediate gratification, patience is an unpopular and seemingly tedious quality. And yet, many studies have demonstrated that those who are able to postpone gratification have greater chance of success in their ventures and in relations with others. Children who can delay immediate gratification (for example, an ice cream cone) in favor of something more substantial later (a bigger ice cream cone tomorrow) show greater intelligence, less risk of delinquency, and better competence in social relationships. They also have a more developed locus of control—that is, a belief that they are in control over their own life, instead of feeling at the mercy of events, powerless, and without a say, the best recipe for depression.

Immediate gratification is one of the most obvious aspects of our contemporary social life. We don't want to wait, we want everything straightaway, and we become aggressive when we cannot have it. In the era of impatience, we have lost the art of waiting. I believe that to rediscover this art and to teach it to our children is to give them one of the best possible gifts.

One of the best ways for doing so is meditation, which can be used as a technique for learning to slow our pace and open our minds to different perceptions of time. It is a means for defeating impatience and eliminating haste. In the Tibetan Buddhist tradition, one meditation exercise consists of filling five hundred little bottles one by one with water—patiently, without hurry. I am filling this little bottle, here, in this moment, without thinking there are 499 to go.

In times when we are becoming more and more impatient, and when our attention is ever more volatile, this could be a great exercise for us all to practice, and to teach in schools.

Patience is not as heavy and tedious as we may think. It is simply a different perception of time. Time inexorably devours our life and robs it of any meaning. Time is our body, which grows old and loses its power; it is ever-impending death, which hangs over and interrupts our life, turns our work to dust, and delivers us forever into oblivion. And so we try not to think about it, but must do as much as quickly as possible before being enveloped by perennial darkness. What a cruel joke. In this perspective, the person in front of us in the line who lingers to chat with the employee about trivial matters, while our time bomb keeps ticking away, cannot help but arouse our murderous instincts.

But what if we were to see our predicament in another way? Perhaps we would discover that time is a mental construct. That there is no need to be afraid or to be in a hurry, because nothing is running away from us. Then perhaps our state of mind becomes calmer, and we see the robbers of our time, big ones and small ones, with a more benevolent eye.

The idea that time is an illusion is variously expressed in all the great spiritual traditions. Maybe this idea is not the monopoly of the enlightened, but more common an experience than we think. One way or another, all of us have had an inkling of eternity. Watching the stars in the night sky, or absorbed in sublime music, or with a beloved person, we may forget the passing of time.

An Indian myth tells of a man who asks Krishna to reveal his *maya*—his illusion. There seems to be no answer to his question, but from that moment, his life, which before had been serene and uneventful, becomes more animated and full of drama. He meets a woman with whom he falls in love, marries, sets up house, works, and becomes rich. Business gets better and better. But then he goes bankrupt, then a terrible flood comes—and just as this catastrophe is about to take his life, he wakes up as if from a dream and sees the divine Krishna smiling in front of him: a mere instant had passed. This whole life full of dreams and nightmares had not taken up more than a moment.

The flow of time is a magical illusion. The sage Ramana Maharshi must have had something like this in mind when, dying, he listened astonished to his disciples' grief: "Where do they think I am going?" When you dwell in the Eternal Now you are not hurrying away to some other place.

All this may seem to have little to do with patience, yet patience is just the ability to face without fear the incessant flow of time. To perceive, in the routine of daily life, surprising flashes of timelessness. Digging deeper, we find that our hurry has to do with our fear of death. If ever we can be free of the need to get there first, do more, earn more, then other people will no longer appear as obstacles to our urgency. We will feel kinder toward them. And we will meet them as human beings, knowing that we have all the time in the world.

GENEROSITY

Redefining Boundaries

One autumn afternoon, I found myself in the midst of a huge storm. Luckily, I had the car. On the way home, I saw a girl caught in the downpour and asking for a lift. I stopped and let her in. When I asked her where she had to go, I found her destination was far from where I lived; but I couldn't leave her in the rain, so I drove her home—and felt rather generous. But when I turned the key to start the car after dropping her off, nothing happened. The rain had damaged the starter motor. Now, leaving the car where I had parked it, I was the one who had to get home in the rain.

The next day, I had to get the car moving again. When I returned, I noticed that it was blocking the road. Someone must have been furious with me, because he had slit one of my tires. I lost much time with the repairs because the mechanic had lots of work, as usual. And as if that were not enough, I found that during that time, someone had called me with an important work proposal. Because I was not there to respond, I had missed the chance.

This everyday horror story suggests that by being generous, we end up paying. If I offer a resource, it might turn out badly for me. I might miss a chance and afterward think, Maybe I would have done better to be more selfish. So what if the girl gets wet in the rain? At least I don't lose a whole morning, as well as time, money, and a good work opportunity.

But that kind of thinking misses the point. The true benefit of generosity, for the giver, is not a material advantage but an inner revolution. We become more fluid, more willing to risk. We place less store on possession and more on people. And the boundaries between us and others become less drastic, so that we feel part of a whole in which it is possible to share resources, emotions, and ourselves.

Surely, to be generous is risky. You cross a line of no return. I remember when my godson Jason, at 4 years old, gave a favorite little toy car to me as a gift. Even though I knew it was precious to him, I accepted it and put it in my pocket. There and then it was all okay, but shortly afterward, Jason realized that to give something as a gift meant to give it away forever. He would never see his toy car again. He had a moment of panic: He wanted it back. It was the panic of losing something immensely precious, without which life would never be the same. Naturally, I was ready to give the toy car back to him. But once his panic was over, Jason decided that I could keep it. He was learning that to give is an irreversible act of commitment. You can't go back once you have leaped into the void.

The weight of what we give varies a lot. We can contribute a bit of our time, a small donation, a book we have already read. Or we can donate our blood or bone marrow, or a huge effort, or a large part of our savings. Whatever the gift, one precondition is essential: To offer, in the moment of giving, all of ourselves. Generosity that is unwilling or cold or distracted is a contradiction. When you are generous, you do not spare yourself.

. . .

GENEROSITY TOUCHES THE DEEPEST STRATA OF OUR BEING.
Whenever we have to deal with our sense of property, we become
touchy. An archaic anxiety pervades our unconscious. It is gener-
ated by millennia of scarcity, precariousness, poverty, and hunger.
Deep within, we are jealous of our possessions, maybe even terrified
of losing them. Why is it so difficult to give what is dearest or what
could be useful to us? It is not only because we know we will miss it,
it is because we fear an irreversible loss. We are losing a part of ourselves. It is like dying.

To be generous means to conquer these old fears. It also means to
redefine our boundaries. For the generous person, borders are permeable. What is yours—your suffering, your problems—is also
mine: This is compassion. What is mine—my possessions, my body,
my knowledge and abilities, my time and resources, my energy—is
also yours: This is generosity.

When we are victorious over age-old unconscious forces, and
when we redefine our boundaries, a profound transformation takes
place in us. But there is no use denying it—even the most relaxed
and cheerful person in the world, in her innermost being, is still attached to her possessions. These emotional muscles are tense. What
is ours, or we believe is ours, we hold tight: a person, a social position, an object, our security. In this holding, there is fear and self-
importance. We are like the children in a Buddhist parable who have
built sand castles on the beach. Each has his castle. Each has his territory. All feel important: "It's mine!" "No, it's mine!" They might
even get into fights, make war. Then evening comes, the children go
back home, forget about their sand castles, and go to sleep. Meanwhile, high tide erases all their creations. Our most precious be-

longings are like sand castles. Do we really want to take ourselves so seriously? Generosity loosens our grip on possessions and allows us to let go.

We have not always been so possessive. Anthropologists tell us that the institution of property as we know it is not the same in all cultures. It was quite different during the paleolithic period. Nomadic societies that still live as we once did—by hunting and gathering—are organized in a way very different from ours. They possess much less, produce much less, and share much more. I wonder how we would appear to such societies—perhaps as a caricature, clinging as we do to our possessions, bent on defending them, counting them, wanting more of them, and envying those of others.

It's a paradox. Covered in a few pieces of hide, out in the cold, surviving in precarious circumstances, exposed to animal predators, collected in small groups—in such a situation, we humans are more likely to be generous and help each other. In a supermarket, in a mildly hypnotic state, with the temperature optimally regulated, with our bank account secure and our stomach full, completely anonymous and surrounded by thousands of stimuli all saying "Touch me! Take me! Buy me!"—in such a situation we are less likely to be generous.

WE THINK OF GENEROSITY AS AN IMPULSE OF THE HEART. Nothing is nobler and more beautiful than someone spontaneously giving. But what kind of giving is it? Generous giving is surrounded by a crowd of imitations. Do we give out of habit, guilt, social pressure? Do we give so as to obtain a tax deduction, or to show off, or because it is good publicity?

In the act of generosity, intelligence also has its say. Sometimes by giving we can hurt or damage. To give a beer to an alcoholic, or a motorbike to a daredevil can be a lethal choice.

A gift can also carry an ideology, or a directive, or a judgment. To give a book of prayers to an atheist, or a gym subscription to an obese person, or a deodorant to someone with body odor is not an example of generosity. These are judgments or pressures disguised as gifts. The giver might object that he or she wants only the well-being or safety or improvement of the receiver. The motivation might be genuine, but the whole operation takes place within the giver's value system. How does the receiver take the gift? Probably with a feeling of discomfort. And besides having to endure the pressure, he is even expected to say thank you. There is no freedom, no heart. Only control.

An act of giving can embarrass the receiver in other ways. It can be a show of superiority and moral grandeur: "See how generous I am." Perhaps the gift is made with the subtle intention of creating a dependence or a debt: "I make this gift, so then I will be able to ask you a favor." Or again, there can be heart but no head. The impulse to give is there, but the gift is cumbersome and useless. How does someone feel who lives in a small apartment and is offered a huge dog? Or a lover of rock music who is made a present of a Beethoven symphony? Many presents are inappropriate and invasive.

And yet each one of us possesses something of interest to others, if not of vital importance: money, time, necessary resources such as water or food, the capacity to give esteem and attention, whatever. Do we wish to share them or not? Our life is made up in such a way that we desire what others have, while we have what others desire—as in a game of cards in which each player has the cards other players need.

True generosity is guided by awareness. It gives people what they really need for their next step forward—which may simply be survival. Or learning. Or developing an interest. Or healing. Or finding work. Or expressing a talent. It is a giving that is not dictated by a sense of guilt, by a debt, by wanting to create dependence or show off. It is truly a free gift, which in turn generates freedom. This is kindness at its best.

You can be generous not only with material possessions, but also with spiritual qualities. Above all, you can be generous with yourself. This is a more subtle form of generosity. All of us have resources of which we are sometimes not even aware. We have ideas, images, experiences, and memories. At times, we are too ready to participate in other people's affairs—we give advice and proclaim our ideas. But often we do not show what makes our heart sing. We keep these experiences to ourselves and communicate only the easy stuff. However, it is through the sharing of our inner life, of the richest and most fertile part of ourselves, that relationships grow rich and enjoyable. Our relationships are defined by how much of ourselves we communicate.

Some time ago, I was interviewed on Australian radio. I have met interviewers who were hurried and inattentive, asked irrelevant questions, or who steered the conversation in order to blow their own horns. One interviewer was not like that. She went to the crux of the matter. From her questions I gradually realized how well informed she was about my work and my books. Bit by bit she dug deeper, asking ever more intimate questions about my inner life, my inspirations, what was dearest to me. The interview was deeply satisfying because I felt I had given the best of myself. At the end I felt extremely well, as after a fine meditation or psychotherapy session.

A few weeks later, the interview was broadcast. Some friends of mine happened to catch it on their car radio. On the road, without expecting it, they heard my voice speaking of intimate subjects and vibrating with emotion. My friends were surprised—not so much at the coincidence of suddenly hearing my voice, but rather at how different I was in this interview from the way I normally was with them. I am usually reluctant to speak about my emotions. I only do it when someone presses me to do so, and then manage as best I can. I have never been a great conversationalist. On that occasion, however, my friends heard me as someone they did not know and whom they liked much more: Why didn't you show us that part of yourself?

Yes, why? Because I did not know I was so interesting. And also because, out of laziness and false modesty, I have tended to be stingy with myself. I did not know I had inside me, like everyone, so many precious goods. All that is dear to us, all that arouses emotion in us, is important and beautiful, not only for us, however talented or untalented we may be, but for other people, too. No life is banal. We are all interesting and, even if we do not realize it, we all have a story to tell. To know we have stories, emotions, ideas, dreams, which are not interesting only to us, but can nourish and inspire many others as well—this is generosity.

We can be generous, too, with our own mental power by offering our thought and attention. When I wrote my first book, I took for granted that some prestigious people would find the time to read it and offer their opinion for quoting on the cover. When I became a little better known and the same requests were made of me, I saw that this job required time and mental energy—two resources of which we never have enough. Then I remembered the corresponding favors done for me, and where I had once seen mere courtesy, I now saw generosity. Our mind can fulfill all sorts of tasks: Give a competent view, examine, reflect, correct a mistake, supply little known but precious information, come up with a brilliant idea. Are we generous enough to take the trouble?

We can also give possibilities. Imagine being in a position to hire staff for your business. Someone arrives who has an unclear past. Perhaps he has just gotten out of prison. He wants to make a new go of life, but who says he will not slip back into his former ways of theft and dishonesty? Are you willing to give him a chance? This too is generosity: You give, at your own risk, the possibility of redemption. Even when we are not dealing with ex-prisoners, we often judge people on the basis of their past behavior. Or perhaps we are willing in our minds to give them the chance that this time might be different. This is generosity of spirit.

We can be generous with work as well. We can do just enough in our job, no extras, like a student who is satisfied with a pass and makes no special effort. Or else we can give more. I was struck once by seeing a cashier at a grocery store open a carton of eggs someone was buying to see if any were broken. No one had asked her to do so. The mechanic who helps you fix your car on his day off, the shop-keeper who tells you where you might find the item of which he is sold out, the teacher who takes the time to give you useful guidance even though he is not required to do so, the doctor who not only prescribes a medicine, but also goes on at length to explain your problem in detail to you—these are all people who give more than they are required to give. They are generous.

IT SEEMS ALMOST OFFENSIVE TO SPEAK ABOUT THE BENE-
fits of generosity. Generosity is, by definition, disinterested. Why should we talk of gain, when being generous is a perfect end in it-self? Only to understand this subject more fully. It is useful to know that generosity is correlated with self-esteem. Those who have high self-esteem tend to be generous, and vice versa: By being more generous, they gain self-esteem. For example, in a study of people who

had volunteered for a risky biomedical experiment, subjects' self-esteem had increased and remained so for twenty years. In a group of fifty-two bone marrow donors, the interviewers discovered in phone interviews that the donors, in the act of donating, believed they were expressing a central trait of their identity and that, as a consequence, their self-esteem had risen.

We know, too, that happier people tend to be more generous. If we are feeling content, we are likely to be kinder to others. Thus, for instance, in a famous experiment, subjects who accidentally found money in a phone booth were more likely to help someone pick up a pile of papers that he had dropped. Someone who is gratified is more apt to feel generous and to help another in difficulty.

But the converse is also true: If you are generous you are more likely to be happy. Generosity is a mood-lifter. As Mother Teresa of Calcutta said to someone who noted the happy, cheerful atmosphere among her team of helpers, "Nothing makes you happier than to help someone who is unwell."

Perhaps we can better understand generosity if we look at examples of false generosity. Think of gifts promised to customers in various commercial promotions: Collect the points, and you will win a magnificent bowl *free!* Everyone diligently collects little stamps and sticks them on the appropriate card, waiting for the day they can have their free bowl. It matters not that the bowl is ugly or that they already have one. What is important is to get something for nothing. As if there were nothing better to do, they patiently, fervently collect their points until the great day. This is a totally fictitious generosity. We all know this is an ingenious commercial device for seizing our attention and winning our business. Yet this ghost, this remote semblance of generosity, fascinates and attracts us.

How sad: There is so little generosity around that the prospect of receiving a little, even when it is not genuine, lures us.

But how wonderful: This very quality is part of our physiology and our ancestry. Generosity is a potential in all of us, so very precious—and so close at hand.

We also know as a documented fact that poorer people, proportionally to their income, give more to charity than richer people. It seems that having little money keeps them more in touch with the values that count, or perhaps it is because it helps them understand the discomfort of lacking what is vital. Or maybe it's because the pain of need keeps alight the flame of compassion. We do not know exactly—maybe poor people donate more money to charity for all these reasons.

When the terrible September 11 terrorist attack took place, most of the world knew in a matter of minutes. But some people heard about it much later. A tribe in South Kenya, in an area remote from Western technology, learned about the attack only seven or eight months later. I do not know how these people, who are not in the least acquainted with our world, imagine it to be, and what they understood about the catastrophe. But they realized a tragedy had occurred. Dressed in their multicolored garments, they held a solemn meeting and decided they would send their most precious possession—sixteen cows—to the people of New York to help them in this difficult moment. These people, who had known the torment of hunger, were now ready to give up their food to show their solidarity to other human beings they had never met.

Generosity is exactly this: to give that which is dearest to us. It is an act that transforms us. After it, we will be poorer, but we will feel richer. Perhaps we will feel less equipped and secure, but we will be freer. We will have made the world we live in a little kinder.

RESPECT

Look and Listen

We all know how it feels to be seen for less than what we are. We feel that we are treated as if we were another person—a poorer, unrecognizable version of ourselves. Our qualities are not perceived, and we are ascribed flaws that are not ours. It is an unpleasant experience that fills us with insecurity and resentment. It happens all too commonly, and simply because people are lazy. Who can be bothered to take the time to know us truly? Very few. It is hard work, too hard. It is much easier to categorize us using some kind of mental shorthand. The unpredictable and the new are ignored because too much effort is required to perceive them.

Even worse is when we are not seen at all—treated as if we were invisible. Life appears to go on without us: People talk among themselves, carry on their usual activities, joke, laugh, eat, daydream, do crossword puzzles, as if we did not exist. In a shop or office, this is normal. At home or with friends, it becomes more worrisome. If it goes on all the time, it is tragic.

Now let us think of the opposite situation, undoubtedly rarer.

Someone has taken the trouble to get to know us and to treat us for who we are. This person recognizes us as real and unique. We are no longer invisible, nor do we feel like a stereotype. Instead, we are an object of interest and appreciation. We feel we have value not just because we respond to a demand, but because of who we are. We are not trapped by someone's low or false idea about us, but we are welcomed as our real selves and seen for what we can become. What a relief! Someone has noticed us. Someone has seen our worth. Someone has seen that we exist.

This is respect—from the Latin *respicere,* to look back, regard, consider. Respect, like patience, may seem a hackneyed, old-fashioned virtue. Yet, if we think about it a moment, we find it holds a store of possibilities. The way we look at others is never neutral, for we transform what we see. We are not like those video cameras in banks and other public places that register everything in an objective, anonymous fashion. In seeing, we give life. Our attention brings energy, while our lack of attention takes it away. Think of the "silent treatment," a form of ostracizing by which the victim is treated as if he did not exist. No one listens to him any longer, no one sees him, no one acknowledges he is there. It is a terrible form of punishment, even though no one lays a finger on the victim or limits his freedom in any way.

In our society, the silent treatment is never deliberately practiced by an entire community on one individual. But even a tiny dose on an individual level can have disastrous effects—destruction of self-esteem, insecurity, depression.

To see, to really see, you need only an instant. I think of the teachers' aide at my son's school who, every morning, greets the children, welcoming them at the door, calling them by name: *"Ciao, Jonathan. Ciao, Cosimo. Ciao, Sofia. Ciao, Irene."* She does not forget a single one. I think of what may happen to a child, instead, who enters a place where no one notices her. She walks in, feeling one of a crowd. She feels she does not count, that she is a nothing. And yet all it takes is for someone to call her by her name, right then, as soon as she steps in. It is like saying: "Here, in this place, you count. Here you are someone."

The Natal people in South Africa greet one another by name, wishing each other good day, but saying, *"Sawu bona,"* which means "Here you are," to which the other responds, *"Sikhona"*—"I am here." They are *seen*.

I FEEL RESPECTED IF I AM SEEN FOR WHO I AM. BUT WHO am I really? Am I what others see in my everyday life? That is just one aspect of myself. It is my façade. If I am sincere and transparent, a lot of me is visible, but it is not the whole lot. So then, who am I? Am I my secret world, with my dreams, my most vulnerable side, which I rarely or never show to others, the fantasies I cannot confess?

We are getting closer, but are not there yet. Am I my unconscious, my shadow—all that is unknown even to myself? Perhaps, but it is not sufficient. Who would like to be known for what is altogether unknown even to himself?

Let's try this: I am that for which I would like to be appreciated and remembered—I am the best of what there is in me, the unique, the loving, the strong. Maybe these traits emerge rarely. Maybe they have never emerged but still could manifest. Sure, I am the reality of my everyday life and feelings—anger, desire, hope, pain. These are my basic, most concrete aspects. But I am also, perhaps above all, that which I could be and which I have not yet been, or have been only in my best moments.

If this part of me is ignored, I am hurt. Thomas Yeomans, author and founder of the Concord Institute, talks of the "soul wound," what we feel when as children we are not seen for who we are—a soul full of marvelous potential for love, intelligence, and creativity—but instead are perceived as a difficult, headstrong child, or as a lovely showpiece, or as a great nuisance—or not seen at all. If the true self is not seen, we are hurt, and this wound will accompany us into adulthood. In order to be accepted, we will cut our ties with our own true soul, with all that really matters to us. Knowingly or unknowingly, we will try to become what others want us to be, or on the contrary, because of our pain, we will be at war with them. Our deep wound will be a remote, opaque reminder that we have lost who we are. Thus, we will survive, but we will not live.

To look is a subjective and creative act. It is subjective because it changes according to how we feel or think in that moment, and according to our past experiences and future hopes. And it is creative because instead of leaving people as they are, it touches and transforms them.

A Middle Eastern story tells of a man who is oppressed by his family. His wife dominates and torments him. His children make fun of him. He feels a victim, and thinks the time has come for him to go away and find Heaven. After much searching, he meets an old sage who gives him detailed directions on how to get there: You have to walk for a long time, but eventually you will arrive. The man sets out. During the day he walks, and that night, exhausted, he stops at an inn to sleep. Being a precise and methodical man, he decides before sleeping to place his shoes pointing toward Heaven so as to be sure not to lose his way the next morning. But during the night, while he is asleep, a mischievous little devil sneaks in and turns his shoes around the opposite way.

Next morning the man wakes up and sets off, this time in the direction opposite to the day before—toward his starting point. As he walks along, the scenery looks more and more familiar to him. He arrives at the town in which he always lived, but he believes it to be Paradise: "How much like my old town Paradise looks!" But since it is Paradise, he feels good there and likes it immensely. He sees his old house, which he thinks is Paradise: "How it looks like my old house!" But since it is Paradise, he finds it very enjoyable. His wife and children greet him: "How they look like my wife and children! Here in Paradise everything looks the way it was before." However, because it is Paradise, everything is beautiful. His wife is a delightful person, his children are extraordinary—they are full of qualities that he, in his daily life, never would have suspected to exist. "Strange, how here in Paradise everything resembles so precisely what was in my life before, and yet everything is completely different!"

We can do the same experiment in our thinking. We choose a person we know well and we think of all her qualities—not only the ones that are most evident to us from our knowledge of that person, but also those that are potential or barely suggested. Maybe we will be able to intuit the person's soul, her deepest and most beautiful kernel. To see the soul is to see the true substance of which a person is made, rather than to stop at the superficial aspects. This is *respicere*, to see truly.

Sometimes these transformations happen by mistake. One day, I was going to lead a workshop and someone pointed out to me Mr. X (a fellow with a white beard) and said, "You can't imagine how funny that guy is! He has a brilliant sense of humor." I looked at him, and he appeared to me like a good-natured elf who went around spreading cheerfulness. Before the group began, I said hello to him, adding, "I hear you have a talent for making people laugh." This small, shy man looked surprised, as if no one had ever told him a thing like that before. During the workshop, I noticed that he seemed pleased, and that he often smiled to himself. I expected him to make jokes, and soon enough he came out with one joke after another, each better than the last. At the end of the morning, I said to the person who, at the start, had pointed him out as having a great sense of humor, "You were right, Mr. X is very funny." To which he replied, "Hang on, whom did you think I meant? I was talking about that guy over there," indicating Mr. Y, a tall, thin man with an annoyed look on his face who had been quiet the whole time.

By calling Mr. X a great humorist, stealing as it were a title for him, I had inadvertently given him permission to express a side of himself that people did not normally perceive or affirm. By way of a chance error, I had seen his hidden quality—and activated it. If I had tried to see in this man a potential to fly or to speak in ancient Persian, he would not have started flying or speaking ancient Persian. But I saw a possibility, and it, by virtue of having been seen, became a reality.

It may seem strange that by changing a thought in my mind I can change a trait in another person. Yet it is only strange if we undervalue the importance of our mind, and if we forget the many ways in which we continually interact. Various studies have demonstrated the Pygmalion phenomenon—if I change my perception of you, you will change. The students who are seen by the teacher as the most intelligent become the most intelligent. The employees who are seen by their bosses as the most competent and efficient *become* the most competent and efficient. Our perception is like a ray of light falling on a plant—it makes it more visible, nourishes it, stimulates its growth. Think of how many talents and qualities in everyone that are not fully manifest because they are not seen.

If these resources are acknowledged, they can be manifest. This is respect. And it is clear that without such respect, kindness is blind—superficial and distracted, unaware of a person's value, and therefore belittling. Not a very substantial kindness.

This careful, penetrating attention changes not only the receiver, but also the giver. Creativity is two-way. If we train ourselves to look at those around us in a more attentive and penetrating way, and to see their most important qualities (perhaps obscured by noisier, superficial aspects), we too will be different. Why? Because we are made of our perceptions. What we see or presume to see day after day constitutes who we are and colors our entire life. If our view is tired and stale and if everything we see appears empty, we will end up empty shells ourselves. If we see people as interesting and special, our world becomes stimulating and open.

We also become more relaxed. In an experiment designed to explore the influence of emotions on the autonomic nervous system, researchers discovered that anger and appreciation produced opposite effects (no surprise here). One group of subjects was asked to conjure feelings of anger, whereas another group was asked to evoke appreciation for other people. In the first group, both heart rate and blood pressure increased. Opposite results were produced in the second group, with a greater parasympathetic activity (which is considered protective) and more coherence in the electromagnetic patterns of the heart.

Appreciating others will make us feel better. In an old Hasidic tale, a monastery is slowly degenerating. The religious fervor is falling. The elders one by one die and are not replaced by younger members. Decadence reigns and, at times, an atmosphere of desperation. One day, a rabbi passes by the monastery. After spending a little time with the monks, he says, "Unfortunately, I have no advice to give you. But remember that the Messiah is among you." Then he goes away. The monks are astonished by this statement. As the days pass, the words continue to resound in their minds. As they look at one another they wonder, "Who is the Messiah among us? Maybe it is that good-natured chatterbox, or that lazybones who never seems to want to do anything, or that quiet, morose one, or else that one who knows everything and always wants to be right . . ." Bit by bit, the faults are seen as qualities: perhaps silence is hiding knowledge; perhaps chattering is a way of keeping people cheerful; or laziness is just serenity. "One of us is the Messiah." And so they treat each other with the greatest respect, with the extraordinary kindness due to a Messiah, that divine being manifest in ordinary guise in everyday life. One of us is sent by God, and we owe him infinite respect.

Gradually this respect felt by the monks (just in case one of them really is the Messiah) transforms their relations and therefore the atmosphere of the whole monastery. They perceive each other in a completely different way—freer and happier. From the outside world, visitors start to come, and then novices. A marvelous spiritual renewal begins in which joy and wonder are reborn. These people learned to see anew and their life changed.

Respect is not just a matter of seeing, however. It is also about hearing. Respect does not exist without a listening ear. This is anything but easy, especially in our noisy world. Never before have we been so beset by sounds that distract and disturb us: traffic, machinery, the inane music we are obliged to hear in restaurants and malls, airplanes flying over our heads or the subway beneath our feet, the neighbors' TV set, or the local rock concert. We are all subjected to noise pollution, noise we have never asked to hear. These sounds enter us, vibrate in us, and little by little do their invisible harm.

Perhaps we make a lot of noise because we do not feel like listening. True listening only happens in silence. I can only hear you when no outside din gets in the way, and especially when I have silenced the inner voices that distract me from what you want to tell me. When we really try to listen, we realize how much we are competing with each other. We might be listening, but meanwhile all manner of thoughts—ideas, words, images—are flooding the screen of our minds, waiting for the other to stop and for the chance to be voiced—and we just can't wait to talk. If we are not interrupting the speaker vocally, we certainly do so with our thoughts.

At times in my workshops, I have used a technique for listening (I don't know who invented it): You put a shell or some other object in the center of the group. Whoever wants to talk takes the shell and says what she wants to say. The others listen, and no one may speak unless he has the shell. When he has finished, he puts the shell back in the center and after a bit of silence, during which everybody digests what has just been said, someone else takes the shell. And so it goes on.

This is a useful technique because it shows us how impelling is our tendency to want to speak ourselves without listening, how strong is our lust for the word. It also shows us how listening forces us to slow our pace, to consider meditatively, because true understanding requires pause and commitment.

Soon enough, though, people grow tired of the exercise. When the shell is back in the center, many race to grab it, and while someone is talking, they are ready to pounce on it, meanwhile thinking of all the important things they have to say. And forgetting to listen.

But listening needs more than just silence. It requires the ability to hear not only what is being said, but *how* it is being said. Often, the words by themselves are not so important, the tone counts much more. For instance, when someone says "yes" to you, is it forced or enthusiastic, sharp or reluctant? Simple phrases like "I'm going for a walk" or "Where did you put the newspaper?" can contain anger, displeasure, protest, affection; we only need to listen. I once saw a painting: A window opening onto a sky full of dark storm clouds, curtains flapping. Underneath were the words: "I don't remember what you said, but I remember how you said it."

Listening is a magnificent art that regenerates and stimulates the beneficiary. He feels at peace because, miraculously, someone is listening without wanting to grab the microphone, or contest what he is saying, or say something smarter, or change the subject. Listening gives value to everything that is being said as well as to the person who says it. In true listening, we hear also what is not patently said. We hear the voice of the soul, maybe its cry.

Listening brings relief also to the listener, because it gives her the peace that comes from silence. To listen, you have to empty yourself of yourself. For a while, your own anxieties and your own troubles do not exist. Inner noise is hushed. While you are listening, you are free.

Thus, respect has as much to do with seeing as with hearing. But if the eyes reveal the soul, the ears would seem not to reveal anything about us; they are the least expressive part of our face. Yet observe their shape, curiously complex, and you will see an extraordinary image of receptivity—the receptivity we often risk losing in our hurried, convulsive lives. The ear is the image of our openness to the world.

The good news is that listening to others is not a boring duty but an interesting adventure, because if we really listen, everyone has something interesting to say, even the people who appear most ordinary.

In an African story, the spider Ananse is given a mission by the sky god to collect all the wisdom of the world and bring it back to him. In exchange, he will be called "the wisest of all time." "No problem," replies Ananse. "I'll do the lot in three days."

He collects all the wisdom in the world and puts it in a large pot. Then, tying the pot to his back, he starts his climb to the sky, scaling very slowly a tall coconut tree whose top is lost in the clouds. When anyone offers him help, he refuses it: He wants to do the whole job by himself, wants to be the one and only keeper of wisdom. He is very proud of his task. From the ground, everyone follows him with bated breath. At the end, Ananse does it: He arrives in the sky with all the wisdom of the earth. He has made it! What a triumph! What happiness! He lifts his eight legs high as a sign of victory. Alas! In doing this, he loses his grip and falls miserably to the ground. The pot breaks and the wisdom ends in a thousand pieces. Everyone wants these precious fragments and runs to get them: They are so interesting, so beautiful! And from that day, no one has a monopoly on wisdom. Everybody has a piece of it. Even the most ignorant, downtrodden, thick-headed, or apparently less gifted have a piece of wisdom. Everyone has something interesting and original to say.

RESPECT IS A NECESSARY CONDITION FOR THE RESOLUTION of conflicts. Fights and tensions are ever-present: In the family, at school, in businesses, among social groups and among peoples. From a banal argument between friends to an atomic war, they are often an absurd waste of time and effort, and the cause of misery without end. Aggression and domination are crude and remarkably ineffective ways to handle problems, generating more harm than they can avert.

When they do not explode in a destructive way, conflicts persist beneath the ashes, sapping energy and resources. For example, in the U.S., sixty-five percent of the problems related to professional output in businesses are due to conflicts between employees; and high-ranking managers in the five hundred biggest American companies spend twenty percent of their time in matters to do with conflicts and litigations.

Conflict resolution can greatly improve relationships and efficiency in businesses. In schools, it can raise the academic standard. To resolve conflicts, the first step is to help the sides state their positions clearly and recognize the point of view and demands of the other. This is respect: the full acknowledgement of oneself and the other. Conflict resolution by way of respect and listening is the most efficient and elegant way to settle disputes. I am not saying it always works, because irrationality, quarrelsomeness, and rigidity abound everywhere. But it is a useful starting point.

WHAT WE HAVE SAID SO FAR CAN BE PUT THIS WAY: RESPECT implies giving to others the space they deserve. We often fail to do this. First of all, we judge. As hasty and biased judges, we quickly reach our conclusions. Even without saying a word, we will form opinions about whoever is in front of us: He is pleasant but deep down presumptuous; she seems nice but is dishonest, and so on. Judging costs nothing. It is quick and easy. It gives us a fictitious sense of superiority over the person we are judging. And whether or not our judgment is correct, it will interfere with the relationship. The other will feel it, be influenced by it, possibly hurt or offended.

Judgment is often linked to the desire to control. We want to give advice, tell the person how to manage his life, save him. How often have you had someone try to tell you what foods to eat, what films to see or books to read, how to use your time, whom to marry or not marry, or what God to believe in? This advice was not merely a way of sharing ideas, but a form of pressure. The underlying idea is that you cannot make it on your own, that you need guidance and improvement.

The mythical image of Procrustes' bed is a perfect example of this idea. This terrible man would make people lie on his bed. If they fit exactly, they were lucky. If they were too long, he would cut off their feet, and if they were too short, he would stretch them till they were the right size. The horror of Procrustes describes well the horror of those who want to interfere with other people's lives. At some time or another, we are all tempted to shape others the way we want them to be.

To understand the damage done by judgment and control of other people's lives, we need to look at an extreme example: the totalitarian regime, in which everyone is regimented, has to dress the same way, read the same books, have the same ideas, wear a beard or mustache, cover her face, or whatever custom is imposed solely in order to control the lives of all. A Romanian musician told me that during the time of the dictatorship in his country, you were not allowed to play jazz—a symbol of decadent American society. You were only permitted to play classical music. If ever he dared to play jazz with a few friends, the police (sent by some informer) would soon arrive and arrest them. If music is the expression of the soul, to repress it is to kill the soul. Here we have one extreme example, and it all started because somebody knew what was best for everybody.

Tolerance is a great virtue. Without it there is no creativity, no love. There is no chance for change or growth—neither in an individual nor in a society. On the other hand, we must not exaggerate. Injustice, bullying, and violence must be opposed. Evil must be faced. Often, as history shows, evil develops because it is ignored.

Thus there is a time for tolerance and a time for zero tolerance. All the same, spacious respect is one of the easiest ways to open up a relationship: Letting other people be what they are without surrounding them, not even in our minds, with judgments, advice, pressure, and hopes that people be this way or that. We do well to trust that they can invent their own destiny. Without this space, kindness is suffocated; with space, it lives and breathes. This is the respect we want to receive. This is the respect we can learn to offer.

FLEXIBILITY

Adapt or Perish

Everything changes. Our body changes. Our ideas change and so do our moods, or the moods of the people we are close to. Our loves and our friendships change. Our finances and our life plans change. The causes of our suffering or happiness change. The political situation changes. Fashion and the weather change. Even change itself changes.

In a universe in which nothing stays the same, it is hard to find any stronghold that may offer us protection and security. The only way to survive consists in the art of adapting to events that continually take us by surprise. If you adapt, you survive. If, in the midst of changing conditions, you stay fixed, you perish.

Every tiny detail in the living world is a hymn to adaptability: The eye of an insect, the plumage of a tropical bird, the fin of a dolphin, the bone structure of a flying fox, the strategy of a reptile, or the functions of the human brain are all testimonies of adaptation to a life in continual change. Those who do not adapt end up like the dinosaurs.

Flexibility and adaptability are characteristics that science and technology have tried to understand and imitate. A good example are the telescopes of the future, based on adaptive optics. Earth's atmosphere is a filter that obfuscates and distorts the images coming from space. The new telescopes, aimed at faraway stars, will take the atmosphere into account, and will adjust their mirrors according to atmospheric perturbations, modifying them infinitesimally hundreds of times a second. In this way, we will be able to obtain precise photographs even of extra-solar planets, which till now have eluded us. It is an invention with its own symbolism: We will be able to see farther, not by overcoming the obstacle but by adapting to it.

In military strategy, the more flexible entity is the one that wins. Thus the English battleships, lighter and faster, had the advantage over the slow, heavy galleons of the invincible Spanish Armada. Adaptability is the secret weapon in the business world, too; there, rigidity is tantamount to defeat. To sell umbrellas during a drought or school texts at the start of vacation has never made anyone rich. Those who are able to sniff out the demands of a market in continual flux survive and grow wealthy.

Flexibility is a form of practical wisdom, an intelligence that lives in the present, that knows how to read the slightest sign of change and then has the facility and pliability necessary for adapting to the new conditions. This kind of wisdom comes from understanding that we cannot control every single element of our existence. To want to master our actual situation is a legitimate desire, particularly if we are surgeons, pilots, or tightrope walkers. But total control over our lives is a fiction—too many unknown variables are at play. If we tried to control every aspect of our lives, we would go crazy—and risk getting the opposite of what we want. It is often wiser to accept the unexpected. If we don't, we are in trouble. It happened to me once.

I was to be interviewed on an important live radio broadcast. My words would go on air with no chance of correction or deletion. It was to be a phone interview, and the very thought of being interrupted by one of my children singing or yelling made me insecure. So I arranged to have the interviewer call me at my office, a quiet room on the top floor, far from both home and traffic noise. When I arrived there, I was told that the plumber was working on the building's pipes, but I did not give it a second thought. After a while, the telephone rang and the interview started. When we reached a crucial part of the discussion, tackling the lofty themes of the spirit, the unpredictable happened: Although I wasn't expecting anyone, the doorbell rang. Ignoring it, I continued talking, but the doorbell kept ringing. It was the plumber. He knew I was in my office and, because I was not responding, advised me by shouting through the closed door, "Dr. Ferrucci, don't use your toilet for the next two hours, or you will make a mess!" The plumber's prosaic interruption went on air at the moment when thousands of listeners were tuned in to hear my profound words. I have no idea what they thought. Did they believe it was part of the show? I was not amused at all by this incident at the time, and only later was able to discover the humorous teaching it offered me. But right there and then I was obliged to realize that much as I tried, I was not in control. The outside world did not adapt to me: More simply and practically, it is I who must adapt to what is happening moment to moment.

THE WORK OF PSYCHOTHERAPY CAN BE DEFINED AS THE recovery, or the learning, of flexibility. We help people who are still facing today's situation with yesterday's strategies. The ways that might have worked yesterday, or at least allowed survival, today are disastrous. Someone abused as a child, for example, lives in constant tension, perhaps closing himself to others like a frightened child. Or else, becoming servile or seductive, he tries to ingratiate himself with a potential enemy. These attitudes, however adequate they may have been in the past, have no more meaning today. Now the danger is over, and the time has come to stop pretending and start living. Another example: Perhaps a parent has devoted many years to the care of children, looked after their health, driven them to school, listened to their dreams and their troubles, given herself heart and soul to their well-being. The children grow up, leave home, and all this work and devotion has to stop—like an obsolete machine that is not useful anymore and is left rusting in a corner. The outer scenario is completely new. Will the inner attitude also change?

The idea is to help all of us recognize present reality. Because, with all its hard, unpleasant invasiveness, reality is our great teacher. Reality proceeds of its own accord, without considering our hopes and dreams. Our fantasies are idle if they do not help us face life as it is in this very moment.

That is why flexibility is not just a successful strategy. It is also a spiritual quality. It implies freedom from attachments, wakefulness in the present, acceptance of what *is*. Changes in our life can be unpleasant, even frightful: the people we love may not love us as before; our professional competence is failing; our body is weakening; our products are no longer selling as they used to; friends who used to give us warmth and support have forgotten us; the activities that once excited us now seem boring and empty.

In the face of continual change, Taoism suggests we be as adaptable as water, which flows over and around rocks, bending its shape to flow on. If we can let go of the beliefs we are most fond of, then we can open to the new, to paradox and the absurd. This is creativity. This attitude becomes a way of life, even a spiritual path. We are able to let go of old models, and we become humble enough to start all over again.

Adapting to the present reality means accepting frustrations. Psychologists have measured the capacity of young children to accept a small frustration—for example, the ability to keep an M&M in the mouth without eating it for ten to thirty seconds; not to look while the experimenter, making a noise with paper, opens a package containing a gift for that child; to look at toys and to choose one without touching anything; to build a tower of wooden blocks with another child, taking turns and not toppling the tower. According to this research, the children who most easily accept the frustration turn out to be the strongest, most pleasant in company of others, most conscientious, and most open to new experiences.

Years later, these children will be adults who will more easily accept the little oppositions so common in everyday life: You can't find a parking spot; the person you are waiting for is late; the computer crashes; the weather is poor and your trip is canceled; the line at the supermarket is ridiculously long; you have to deal with boring bureaucracy; and so forth. Reality knows nothing of your plans, and it comes up with ever-new ways to pester you. According to recent research, you are bound to meet twenty-three frustrations today (up from thirteen a decade ago). Will you fight or will you dance?

The ability to be flexible resonates in our relationships. We may be endowed with warmth and goodwill, but if we do not adapt to the new, we will be stressed, in a bad mood, irritated, hostile, or overwhelmed by a situation we do not expect, and will therefore have less mental and emotional energy for expressing the best of ourselves with others. We will be only half there. The other half will be battling, grumbling, resisting.

Because flexible people accept what is, they are easier to be with. With whom would you prefer to dine—someone who complains if there are no prawns flambé, accompanied by a '67 Riesling, or someone else happy with a plate of pasta and beans? Who would make a better guest—a friend who is grateful for a good night's sleep and who, with no particular demands, manages independently in your home, or a relative who needs your company all the time, complains that the mattress is too hard, and requires you to help him find an expert in Japanese stamps? No doubt about it: Easygoing people are a blessing.

Desires and demands are the arena in which a relationship is put to the test. If the needs are normal and legitimate, and if they are reciprocally recognized and satisfied, all is well. The relationship works. But imagine that needs become urgent, capricious demands. The relationship then becomes difficult. More than easily strolling in the countryside, it feels like rafting down the rapids.

But lo and behold, excessive and arbitrary requests may not be what they seem. In fact, they often are a distraction because they make us evade what is most important in a relationship—to see each other as we are, to communicate, and to get along well together. Many people who are secretly afraid of intimacy erect a barrier between themselves and the other, a barrier made of continuous demands and impositions. There is a cartoon of a woman who has received an engagement ring with a gem, who examines it with a magnifying lens. In that moment, she couldn't care less for her fiancé. All she sees is the diamond. At the other extreme of this continuum, imagine a person content with little: "I don't need anything—I am happy just to be with you." What a sigh of relief.

Besides the active demands, the ones we express aloud, the passive ones are also ready to create havoc. They are the demands we take for granted and deliberately do not express. One of the most common is, "I expect you to be always the same." Usually, even if we express the hope that people around us change, we are all prone to perceptive inertia: We continue to perceive them in the same way, and unconsciously want them to stay the way we see them. Anything that might conflict with our fixed idea of a person will annoy us.

We expect those around us to continue being what they were. We label them, and then keep them in a mental box. As a psychotherapist, I sometimes receive calls from a client's relatives protesting that she is changing—perhaps becoming more assertive, or bringing to light a new trait; life with her is becoming less easy. All they want is for the client to stop suffering, and stop causing suffering to others, but they fail to realize that in order for that to happen, that person has to change. And when she does not correspond any longer to the image they have of her, they get upset. I still remember a father's disdain and surprise when his daughter, till then depressed, inert, obedient, decided to leave her job and take a trip around the world. His daughter had changed, she was achieving her freedom. But her father was holding on to the past and fighting the novelty with all his cannons.

It happens to everyone. One evening at a restaurant, instead of the usual plate of pasta and vegetables with mineral water, I ordered a pizza with sausage and a glass of beer. You should have seen my family's reaction: They considered me perverse, an individual without taste, a lost soul destined in the future to cope with serious health problems, though if anyone else ever ordered the same, they would have made nothing of it. They simply could not bear the dissonance with the image they had made of me, and found it hard to think of me breaking out of those confines. Are we an especially rigid family? I don't think so. We are normal. But I vote for liberty. The ideal is a world in which older children and their parents reciprocally give permission to one another to dye their hair, attach any ring to any part of their body they want, follow their sexual preferences, dress as they desire, spend their money as they deem best, choose whatever chemical substance they wish to introduce into their organisms (well, with a few exceptions), change their personalities, and suddenly depart for distant and mysterious lands.

To give the people we love the freedom to be what they want to be. To give them the space to experiment, make mistakes, be creative, fail or succeed. To allow them to discover their thousand faces without freezing them in the immutable mold of our beliefs. Without protecting, preaching, pushing, or pulling accordingly to what we believe is best. What a great way to relate. Would you not want others to trust you and treat you this way?

Generally, we imagine that the older we are, the more rigid we become. But it is also true that children are creatures of habit and often dislike change. And I happen to think that we ought to respect their need for structure. I once tried to surprise my goddaughter, whom I had not seen for a year, by hiding in a wardrobe and popping out suddenly when she entered the room. The joke did not please her at all, and she ran away crying. She was right: Godfathers do not come out of wardrobes. Children need fixed points of reference. You don't take flexibility too far.

With adults, however, it is a different question. If we manage to relax our rigidity and not take our expectations too seriously, we will give space to others to be what they want to be: to express new ways of thinking and acting, to show us unexpected sides of themselves, and perhaps to mature. If you enter into a relationship with someone secretly expecting he will stay the same (because, after all, you are used to it this way), then you will be relating with a subscription or with an insurance policy—not a real person. The more chance you give him to change and experiment, the more the relationship will become an adventure in which you both wonder what the next step may be.

The family, too, can be more or less adaptable. It can adjust to moments of stress, to changes, and to difficult periods in childhood and adolescence. Studies show that the greater the adaptability of the family during the children's adolescence, the better will be their intimate relationships when they are adults.

If we are flexible, not only do we adapt more easily to others' changes, but we will better manage the difficult task of yielding without getting depressed or angry. To yield may mean, for instance, to acknowledge that another person knows more than we do, to say sorry for a mistake, to acknowledge our wrongs, to give way to others. Have you ever found yourself at an intersection or in a lane where not a single car would slow down to let you in? Maybe I was one of those drivers. When I drive, I sometimes yield to other drivers, but other times I don't, and then (I have come to realize) I need to justify it to myself. I will say to myself that I am in too much of a hurry to stop, or that the other driver was advancing too aggressively, or that if I did stop to let him in, I would risk being bumped from behind. And yet, think about it: How does it feel when all the cars keep moving in front of you and pretend you are not there, or maybe even accelerate a bit to close the space available and prevent you from edging in? And how does it feel when someone stops to let you in, and maybe even smiles? That is what kindness feels like.

Driving is perhaps the arena in which it is hardest to yield. I still remember a distressing scene I witnessed a few years ago on one of the narrow roads in the hills around Florence, where two-way traffic is impossible. Two drivers came opposite each other. Usually, one driver would yield and reverse to let the other pass. But this time neither would do so. They stopped to argue. The more they stated their reasons, the less they were willing to give in. They were both wasting time and holding up others by blocking the road. Worse still, they were harming their own well-being.

Yielding is not easy, though we may know it is often the right choice and works best. Our culture prizes self-affirmation and views yielding as a weakness and a defeat. It is what we often see in political debaters, who have a terror of appearing incompetent. Actually, the ones who at all costs want to appear strongest are usually the weakest, and at times they look ridiculous or pathetic. Comics have sometimes expressed this fact with great humor. I am thinking of a famous scene in Chaplin's *The Great Dictator,* in which Hitler and Mussolini have no other way to show their superiority over each other than by sitting at an ever higher level. Eventually, by elevating their chairs more and more, they end with their heads against the ceiling.

The nicest aspect of being flexible, and the one that has most to do with kindness, is perhaps availability. People vary immensely in the degree to which they possess this quality. Some hide behind answering machines, impersonal assistants and waiting rooms, lines and waiting lists. Sometimes they are very important people and the waiting is justified. But I suspect that often it is a front to make you feel, by their extraordinary unavailability, that they are much more important than you are. I once asked to see a literary agent whom I would have liked to handle one of my books. The secretary made a fuss, then told me I would have to send a detailed biography, and that after a few months the agent would "concede" me an interview. That "concede" just sounded too patronizing so I dropped the matter. Just as well. The agent I have now is always available, and when it comes to selling my books, she is dynamite.

To be available can of course be tiring and can open the door to people who exploit us and waste our time. Also, many of us are loaded with work. We cannot respond to every request, return every call, satisfy every need, answer each e-mail. But this is not a matter of physical impossibility. It is a matter of holding an inner attitude of availability as a guiding value in dealing with others.

A little more kindness and good organization goes a long way to making people feel welcome. I have seen doctors who make you wait in overcrowded waiting rooms in the company of other distressed patients, some given to violent coughing or loud lamentations, so that when at last it's your turn to see the doctor, you are sicker than you were before and can't wait to get out. And I have seen people who can be available straightaway, and will meet you just because you are there and need them in that moment.

I know a violin-maker in Florence (her studio is behind the Palazzo Vecchio). She is famous for the extraordinary quality of her violins and has served some of the world's best violinists. Yet if I bring her my son's little violin to fix, she drops what she is doing and fixes it in a few minutes. In another field, I know a man called Fulmine ("Lightning"—believe me, his true name) who started a shutter company. I called him once and spoke to the secretary. After giving my details, I asked when he would be able to come and fix my shutter, hoping to hear something like, "In a few days." The secretary's reply was, "He's already on his way."

Now that's what I call availability.

MEMORY

Have You Forgotten Anyone?

You walk down the street and suddenly meet a person you haven't seen for twenty years. You don't know all the trials and tribulations she has gone through during this period. In some part of your brain, you still preserve the memory of that person as she was a long time ago. Like a wax figure in your gallery of memories, she has remained what she was then—in your mind. Unexpectedly, you face her. As if in a horror film, she seems to have aged suddenly. Uncanny. It is as if someone had turned the handle of the time machine, and all those years had gone by in a flash. In this brusque way, life gives us a shaking and reminds us that time passes, that nothing will ever be the same.

Thus one fine autumn morning I meet my old English teacher. For a period, many years ago, she had held a place in my life: I saw her once a week for our tedious English lessons. Then we moved and I lost touch with her. Now, without warning, I stumble upon her at the market. I recognize her first. She has grown whiter and heavier, but I would say she has aged decently. I tell her my news, and ask hers. At this, her face saddens. She says, "We stopped at W." At first I do not understand. Then I remember: This woman was writing an Italian–English dictionary with her husband. They were compiling it the old way, artisan style. They proceeded one letter at a time. For a while, they would immerse themselves in the A, for example, and in their lives at the time only words beginning with A would count; then the B, and so on. They had just begun the project when I had seen her last.

Already at D, her husband was showing signs of deterioration, but they were not too worried. At the I, there had been an interval of sanity, but meanwhile the sickness was invisibly advancing. The L had been lethal. At that time there had also been a car accident. The P was a time of pessimism and failing health, during which her husband had to go to hospital. S was the time of suffering and sorrow, and so on, from bad to worse, letter by letter, up to W. The writing of the dictionary, already slowed down, stopped at her husband's death. She had not been able to go on after that. The work was interrupted, the dictionary left unfinished.

I find this way of remembering life events by the letter quite strange, and yet I ought not be surprised, since all of us, in our minds, connect the milestones of our existence with our thoughts and emotions. But what strikes me most is this woman's pain continuing through the years and my obliviousness to it. I had gone on toward new experiences, and I had forgotten her. Meanwhile she had suffered. She had moved, with painful slowness and a tormented soul, through the pages of her dictionary, and in the end had remained alone.

Yes, people are still there even when we do not think of them. They continue to suffer, work, enjoy, get sick, get well, die. This is an undeniable and obvious fact. But are we really convinced? To our narcissistic mind, other people exist only when we see them, touch them, hear them, or at least think about them.

When we meet these people after many years, we are surprised to find that life has gone ahead for them too. Perhaps we also feel guilty for having forgotten them. My English teacher had continued her existence from A to W with huge upheavals. I, swept along by life, had gone in a different direction. I could not have eliminated her suffering. Yet, who knows, by the occasional phone call or visit, I might have alleviated it, might have given her the feeling that she was not alone, that there was someone in the world who remembered her. But it did not happen that way.

Many people in our lives seem to grow obsolete. For a while they are useful, interest us, stimulate us. Then they lose their importance and we forget them. This process is reinforced by the prevailing attitude of our times, which conjures for our benefit an illusory world, where rhythm is fast, feelings shallow, and satisfaction guaranteed. We live in the spurious present—a present unrelated to past or future. It is the present of consumerism, in which we incessantly look for new products and get rid of the old ones.

This is the throw-away style. What we do not need, we dispose of. Cynical as this may sound, this attitude is, with subtler and less brutal variations, carried over to human relationships We forget the people we are no longer interested in. Often these are elderly people, but they can be of any age. This is rarely an explicit way of thinking: We are busy and hurried, rushing around, unable to fulfill all our commitments, and cannot be expected to spend time on those who, seen from our busy perspective, seem irrelevant. Like cars in the fast lane, we accelerate and leave the slower vehicles behind. Or else *we* are the slow ones, watching others overtake us then disappear in the distance.

The case of old people is telling. If you go to Alaska, you will find that, in the traditional way of life, the elderly Inuit are respected and revered because they are the ones who know where to make the hole in the ice for finding fish and surviving. If you visit tribal Nigeria, you will learn that to be old is an honor, because only the elderly have the right to counsel and to heal. In traditional India, you find that old age is the stage of life dedicated to spiritual life and to rising above mundane ambitions and preoccupations. Here in the West, things are different. The elderly are often forgotten, they lose their importance and vigor, and fade away in our memory and in the real world. In the worst scenario, they are unnecessary. I once asked a group I was teaching to say the first words they spontaneously associated with "old age." The most common responses: "Alzheimer's," "incontinence," "weakness," "senility," "coffin."

ANOTHER SIGN OF OUR TIMES IS THE USE OF THE WORD "memory" as an analogy. You hear that certain materials can keep a particular shape: That is their "memory." The material of my trousers "remembers" the right crease, "forgets" the wrong one. Computers have a memory, and we take great pains to save all our data, in case the computer loses its memory. My tax man saves all the data in his office every single evening. His job depends on that. I heard about a man whose computer lost all the memory of his business: addresses, transactions, accounts, and so on. The man was so upset that he grew sick and died soon after.

We, too, feel at times like bad imitations of a computer, and worry when we cannot remember names and telephone numbers. But is this true memory? Not so, in my opinion. The essence of memory is not in the storage of information, but in the emotions we hold, in the meaning we give to our recollections, in relationships that, because we remember them, stay alive. The friends of my childhood, the pain of a goodbye, the meeting with a special person, a wonderful September afternoon, and so forth—all these are not merely items I keep in an archive. They are vital ingredients of my history. Through my memories I build my life and my identity. I am what I am by virtue of how I remember what has happened to me, the people I have met, the mistakes I have made, the triumphs I have enjoyed. I remember, therefore I am.

To remember is to live. To forget is to die. When someone who is no more lives in our memories, he is suddenly present again. A woman who used to know my mother once told me a few things about her, years after her death—things I did not know. My mother had helped her in a moment of need, had confided in her, had also spoken about me. Thus, unexpectedly, my mother was present again. When someone dies, the best way to help those who loved her is perhaps to recall episodes in her life. In memories we preserve the soul. By remembering, we can win a small victory over the inevitability of death.

But it is often easier to forget. What we forget is far bulkier than what we remember. Our memory is sternly selective. We think about the people who are useful to us, and let the others go. We can rummage about at will in our memories. But in our archives there are many we will never again retrieve. Thus we can discern a basic attitude, rarely explicit, toward other people. To put it bluntly, there are A-grade and B-grade people: those who count, who are useful, entertaining, pleasant, helpful to us; and even if we may not admit it, those we consider less useful or pleasant. To take this attitude toward others to its logical extreme is a subtle form of violence. To ignore and forget someone is invisible violence, accomplished without punches and shooting. Yet it is still violence, since it pushes the person into the realm of loneliness and irrelevance.

Fortunately there is another way of regarding others. It is to think of everybody as equally important, equally valuable. In his wonderful book *Albert Schweitzer's Mission: Healing and Peace,* Norman Cousins tells about the time he went to meet Albert Schweitzer. He had with him a letter to Schweitzer from a child, and he gave it to him. It asked advice about music. After Schweitzer read the letter, the two men discussed various subjects of great importance: world peace, relations between the United States and the USSR, missiles and atomic weapons, medicine and witchcraft, healing, human relations—all universal themes. This meeting was to have concrete effects in easing world tensions and starting détente. At the end, Schweitzer came back from the universal to the particular. He remembered the boy and wrote him a letter. The child was as important to him as Kennedy and Khrushchev. In this view no one is left out, everyone is important.

To be forgotten because we do not count is devastating. It is social exile. To be remembered, valued, taken into consideration like everyone else, makes us feel worthwhile. But the act of remembering is beneficial also to those who remember. To live in a state of amnesia, to live without history, is lethal because we no longer know who we are. In the novel *Nuova grammatica finlandese* (New Finnish Grammar) by Diego Marani, a man is found with his cranium half smashed, taken to hospital, and is healed. However, he has lost his memory. Not only does he not know who he is, but he does not know what language he speaks. He has no identity. A few clues suggest that perhaps he is Finnish. Thus he begins to study Finnish and tries to reconstruct his identity. It is a long and exhausting job, carried out in darkness because the memory is lost forever. At the end, the protagonist discovers by chance that he is not Finnish at all. The clues had been misinterpreted. But it is too late. He is now part of the Finnish army, to fight a war for a country that is not his, without knowing who he is.

We can look at this story as a metaphor of our lost memory, for we are all in some way amnesic. In this age, the world moves ahead so fast it is hard to keep track of all the news. We are continually distracted by new stimuli, and the present is re-created daily—through events, people, fashions, ideas, buildings, places, objects. Everything lasts a short while, then vanishes. Since the rhythm of change is so quick, we scarcely stay in contact with the people in our lives. Each one goes his or her own way in a lifestyle far more complex and varied than it was, say, a hundred years ago. The danger is that we even lose contact with ourselves, with the continuity of our own history. And then we try to form an identity for ourselves, like the man in the story, but it is a fiction, therefore weak. And finally, we do not even know who we are.

There are some partial remedies. In my work as psychotherapist, at the start of my meetings with clients, I ask them to write their autobiography. The memories they produce are often partial, bringing with them forgotten emotions, resentments, and hurt they no longer wish to face. Areas of unconsciousness persist. Bit by bit, a person can become conscious of his own history because everyone's life is a coherent narrative, even if we perceive it as an untidy mixture of unfinished events. Bit by bit we can make peace with our own existence, understanding that our history makes us who we are and determines what we can do. Our memories, the lessons we have learned, the difficulties we have overcome, our successes and failures, the people we have known: All this is part of our life, all helps us know that we are who we are.

A client of mine wanted to explore her identity by reconstructing her childhood. She had grown up in a small town in the Austrian mountains, where her parents had left her in the care of nuns from the age of two. It had been very hard. At forty, my client returned to the place, of which she had but the most fleeting memory, and found scattered among various other towns three out of four of the nuns who had looked after her (one had died). With the help of photographs, she was able to reconstruct those years. The sisters still had a clear memory of her. Thus it was a powerful encounter. After this exploration, my client felt different. She had restored continuity in her life. She felt stronger and more real.

Experts talk about "autobiographical memory," and believe that we are continually rewriting our history, reassessing it according to the more or less comprehensive image we have of ourselves. Furthermore, memory serves as a social glue. We feel close to people who have in common with us memories of a time gone by. To be in the present, as we saw in an earlier chapter, is essential. But to have memory is just as essential.

If we are in touch with our history and have made peace with all the difficulties we have found on our way, we feel more grounded. If, on the other hand, we live in a state of amnesia, divorced from our past, if our history weighs on us or poisons us, or if we have lost it altogether, then we may have a harder time. Our past is baggage we carry on our journey. We will be going into unknown territories, perhaps beautiful but nevertheless dangerous, where anything is possible. Maybe we carry a bag full of useless, heavy stuff, slowing us down and making us stop every few paces to catch our breath. Or we have no baggage: We travel light, but without knowledge of where we are going, where we came from, and without supplies of food or drink. Or else we have a light backpack, containing only essential items: food and drink, sleeping bag, detailed maps, travel notes, a compass.

Some memories can never be erased. The dawn of our past is perhaps what counts most of all, what remains most impressed in our cellular memory, even if we forget it. What was our primary relationship like—usually the one with our mother, the person who guaranteed our survival, protected and took care of us? Many aspects of our personality depend on this relationship. Moreover, our experience of this vital relationship determines how we relate to our own children. Imagine having before you a couple expecting a child. You want to know what kind of relation they will establish with the child to be. What is the best predictor of this relationship that has yet to take form? Is it how they respond to a test? A personality inventory? Their philosophical or religious beliefs? The relationship between the two of them? None of the above. The crucial and most important factor is the way the two parents-to-be describe their own relationship with their parents. What once was in their life probably will be repeated in that of their child.

If we now look at another life circumstance, we find a curious and striking example of how our past is part of us. It is the near-death experience. Many people who have nearly died and returned to life describe their experience in surprisingly similar terms. Many remember having seen their entire existence in a single moment, or else having traveled along a dark tunnel toward a preternatural and sublimely beautiful light. Finally, many recall meeting their dear ones who had died before and who have come to meet them, to help, guide, and comfort them. This meeting is exactly what we need at such a moment. It is moving and healing.

Are these beings really the souls of our departed ones? Or is this an emergency reaction of our organism, an explosion of endorphins that, by way of beneficial chemistry and reassuring images, allow us to cope with extreme stress? For our purposes the answer doesn't matter, because both explanations leave one point intact: The people who belong to our history are part of us, and we need their presence and support in order to feel strong and whole.

Some people, therefore, are alive in our view of the world, in our cells, our identity, whether we like it or not. Others are less important, or at least so it seems. But all, even the less important, have participated in our history and have made us the person we are now. They are like the roots of a tree—the smallest and farthest counts too.

Acknowledging our roots changes us. It makes us feel truer. Many people are interested in their family history, an interest that comes from the fear of not having roots, of standing on emptiness. But even more important than investigating our ancestry is rediscovering the connections with those who have crossed our path.

Every parent knows. Take any milestone in a child's life: the first steps, a birthday, a school play, a holiday. Inevitably you will find a parent intent on photographing or filming the scene. Also, children insatiably demand from their parents and other relatives stories of their own childhood. They have a great curiosity about what they were like and what they did, and they like to hear memories told over and over again. This is because they need to piece together a story, their own story—they have to make a complete human being out of themselves. Parents' taking of photographs and telling of stories are so widespread as to seem universal, so automatic as to seem instinctive—like feeding and protecting their children. Preserving memories helps give children a sense of identity and the strength that comes with it. If you know where you come from, it is easier to decide where you are going.

Memory is also social. There are places and landscapes where the memory of a people lives, and this is true not merely for ancient societies, but for everyone. It holds, too, for festivals, rites, music and song, tales, customs. They are a patrimony worth preserving. The same goes for language, a true masterpiece of human intelligence, to which countless individuals have contributed through the centuries. And what about food, perhaps the most direct link with a culture? Food contains a world of emotions. Like language, food is the result of a gradual evolution: The best dishes have always survived their many variations and experiments. You eat food, and you get in touch with a way of feeling and tasting life.

Yet landscapes are often disfigured by ugly new buildings; traditional music, stories, and customs risk dying forgotten; language is becoming impoverished; traditional foods are replaced by mass-produced, nondescript dishes to be eaten in nondescript places. This process favors profit and efficiency, but it generates a world that is colder and without character, a present that is already dead before being born. This is an enormous problem in our contemporary world.

This reminds me of a little story. One day in the center of Florence, a young woman addresses me, "Hey, you, where's the Mac?" She meant McDonald's. Behind her hung a group of famished kids, all like her, who looked like they had to sink their teeth into something—fast. In that moment, I understood the importance of preserving the past. What a gaping lack of respect it is to carry on with our lives, ignoring what the people who lived before us said and did, how they suffered, what they created, and even how they ate. And those who take the trouble to preserve the most creative and beautiful heritage that our predecessors left us are performing an act of kindness. The famished kids want to wipe it all out in one stroke by swallowing a plate of mass-produced, impersonal food. No, young woman, I forgot where the Mac is, but I know a place where they make great pasta.

What is the relationship of kindness to memory? A small experiment is enough to see. Think of the people you have lost along the way—the ones who are not so important—and note your reaction at recalling them: gratitude, resentment, guilt, happiness, pity, indifference. . . . In what way are they part of your life?

We cannot be kind if we forget those who are no longer useful to us. We will never be whole and comfortable, in ourselves and with others, if we divide people into grade A and grade B. We will not understand the relationships we have with one another if we do not deeply understand how much our lives are woven together in the past, present, and future, how much they become part of one another, and how much each one of us is everyone else.

LOYALTY

Don't Lose Your Thread

Some time ago in southern Italy, a violent earthquake shook to pieces a number of houses built just a few years before. Made for quick profit and badly constructed, at the first tremor they collapsed into dust. Other houses, which had been built eight centuries before by the Normans, enjoyed a better fate. They were created to last, to provide a safe and comfortable living space, and they stood intact.

Relationships are like that. The ones that exist only for someone's advantage—money, pleasure, social contact, prestige—have fragile foundations and last only as long as their originating motive survives. Others have a long, healthy life, like the Norman houses, because they are built to last and because the people who began them are not concerned with immediate advantages. Thus, at the first tremor—financial trouble, sickness, failure, personal difficulty—they remain firm and even become stronger than before. In these relationships, what counts most is not extracting from another a tangible benefit, but the peculiarly good feeling that comes from giving presence, support, and friendship over time to a person, whatever may happen and even against one's own advantage. It is right to do so. This capacity to last even in difficult and uncomfortable moments is an essential ingredient of kindness. It is called loyalty.

Let us now imagine a person who is fully in contact with her own feelings and memories. She did not accept blindly her ideas and principles, but gathered them bit by bit, by reflection and conscious choice. She knows what really counts in her life and fights to achieve it. She faces frustration and pain with courage. Such a person has the prime material needed to be loyal. She has substance.

In fact, there is really no such thing as a person without substance. But many people do not know, recognize, or respect the value they have inside them. This is because they have been hurt and prefer to live superficially, where they are less likely to be seriously hurt. These people easily change their minds with fashion or circumstance. Their relations are short-lived because they are based mainly on private gain. They are opportunistic.

This is not a question of good versus bad, but rather of strong versus fragile. Some individuals have retained their integrity, and for them it is natural to be faithful and trustworthy. They know how they feel, what they want, and what they believe in. Their loyalty has roots in fertile ground, and grows from clarity and inner strength.

People who are not loyal find it terrifying to look into their own feelings—they are afraid of what they might see. To have their own ideas is frightening; they would expose themselves too much. Their self-esteem is too low, so they have to survive like beggars, asking for support here and there, wherever they may find it. They lack security and character, therefore it is much harder for them to be loyal.

When we lose the strength to take a risk and to commit ourselves, we live on the surface. Our life is chaotic and senseless. Dante depicts the slothful in hell—those who cannot decide, who cannot be faithful to an ideal or a person—as individuals who are obliged to run continuously behind a banner. The punishment symbolizes in caricature what they ought to have done when alive: truly commit themselves. It is an enormous army of people, and Dante shows greater respect even for the sinners who have done wrong, yet who at least had their own ideas to which they were faithful. Among the slothful there are also the angels who, when Lucifer had committed the sin of pride against God, did not take a stand. They are all beings without faith, without substance, so numerous according to Dante that they populate the world.

We would all like to be associated with loyal people. Nevertheless, we do not hear much about this quality. Loyalty, of all the qualities, is the least fashionable. There are no studies on it, though research on "brand loyalty" abounds. This itself is a phenomenon that is a symptom of our times and bears examination.

"Brand loyalty" is the tendency of a consumer always to use the same brand of a product. The word "loyalty" is totally justified because we tend to form an emotional bond to a product. We all know people who are enthusiastic about their cameras, or who get excited at the mention of their favorite car, or who cannot live without clothing of a famous designer. This is not so much about the quality of the product. It is the brand that counts because it stands for a way of being and a style. And perhaps it also offers the guarantee of belonging to a group.

Furthermore, the brand has a magical ability to encompass faculties and powers that all of us would like to have. Buy these shoes and you will feel like you have wings on your heels. Buy this liqueur and you will be part of the aristocracy. Buy this perfume and the beauty of a goddess will be yours. It is easy to see how the sellers of a product will seek every way of gaining our loyalty and are thus prepared to promise anything to get it. The consumer has to continue to give money to *them* and not to their competitors. And the longer the link with consumers lasts, the more it is reinforced. It starts early: Brand loyalty is skillfully elicited from childhood so that it will remain a constant in future years.

Brand loyalty is not at all a superficial phenomenon. I am convinced that it is based on our desperate need to trust someone or something, to love and to be loved, to gain stability, protection, belonging, meaning. This is why we grow fond of a brand, and this is how the need is exploited commercially. This is why we go about collecting points, wearing clothing, watches, hats with their labels showing, offering free brand advertising. This is why we prefer an emotional gain to a tangible, practical one. We *need* to be loyal.

Why this great need? The answer is simple: because the continuity and stability of relationships have become a rarity. We live in the Age of Distraction, which is also the Age of Interruption, and we are continually invited to think of something other than what we were thinking about. The most significant symbols of this age are perhaps the TV remote control and the telephone. The remote control allows us to go from one subject to another—from a love story to the atrocities of war to a diaper ad—with minimal effort. The telephone, especially the mobile, has the magical power to interrupt any relationship or activity—an act of love, a concert, a family dinner, a religious function—with imperturbable impudence: "I couldn't care less what you are doing. Now you listen to me." And that is not all. We can use call waiting and start a telephone conversation, interrupt it, start another one, and finally choose the one we like more. The advertising that launched this service in Italy has become famous: A girl flirts with two boys at the same time, while each of them thinks he is the one and only. A perfect image of disloyalty.

The girl is unpleasant because she is false. But she is also amusing and seductive because to live on the surface allows us, in case we are rejected or hurt, to keep our options open.

Distraction causes continuous loss. "What were we talking about? I have forgotten. Anyway, it doesn't really matter. I have lost the thread, so I'll just change the subject." Thus interruption levels and trivializes our interactions. When I interrupt you, I bring you down to my level, making you my equal. Interruption has probably always been around, but in contemporary times, the greater superficiality, new technology, and acceleration in almost every field have hugely encouraged it. I suggest that the Age of Interruption really began when Coleridge was writing "Kubla Khan." He was in a state of creative reverie, visualizing a continuous flow of marvelous images and poetic thoughts, when an unexpected business acquaintance arrived: the intrusion of prosaic life into the world of poetry. Coleridge lost the thread and never managed to finish the poem the way he had conceived it. Two centuries later, René Daumal, sick in bed, had almost finished writing his masterpiece, *Mount Analogue*. In this novel, the ascent of the mountain is a metaphor for spiritual elevation. The protagonist had just arrived on the summit and was about to find full enlightenment, but someone knocked at the door and Daumal was interrupted. He never finished his book. Not long after, he died.

Indeed, we live in times of multiplied distractions and interruptions. And we live in times when our need to be faithful does not find expression in a relationship but is twisted and exploited for commercial ends. It is a way of living in which we risk losing continuity of relations through time. We lose the thread.

Loyalty is the exact opposite. It is a "being with." It consists in keeping the thread, without allowing distraction or interruption to guide our lives. It is honoring what counts most, and continuing to do so despite the obstacles. A writer I know once recounted this curious episode to me: He had met a scientist, a man of great culture and intellectual vitality. Their conversation, highly varied and stimulating, was interrupted by a huge storm. The two of them parted at great speed in two taxis. Five years later, they met again by chance. Without even greeting the writer, the scientist took up the thread of their conversation at the exact point where they had been interrupted five years before. Faithfulness and loyalty do the same, not only with the mind, but also with the heart.

I remember when, as a boy, I went to America with my family. In those days, the 1950s, you went by sea. We were going for only a few months, but there was also a group of emigrants leaving forever. The passage between continents was infrequent and costly. Not an everyday matter, to go to America. The ship unmoored and left, moving very slowly, and a band on the wharf played heart-rending music. From the ship, we could see the families of the emigrants waving goodbye, knowing they would not see one another for many years, possibly ever again. I will never forget their faces. Yet in that immense sadness, you could see great strength. Though I have no proof, I am sure those families were capable of lasting relationships. I am sure that after twenty or thirty years, their affections, having passed through who knows what vicissitudes, would have remained unchanged.

As you part, so are you reunited. In an exceptional event reported in the papers a few years ago, a select group of citizens from North Korea had permission, after about fifty years, to see their families in South Korea again. Sons, daughters, and parents, aunts, uncles, nieces, and nephews who had been separated in the forced division between North and South Korea were allowed to meet for a few hours in a large room. The photographs, showing the expressions of highly intense emotions, said more than any research or study can convey. They stated so strongly that the deepest affections, when not repressed or ignored, are anchored in the heart and last a lifetime.

Let us now return to our previous question: Why do we experience such a deep need for loyalty, and even in the Age of Distraction continue to seek it? One possible answer is that loyalty has ancient, prenatal origins. Loyalty is linked to our relationship with our parents, especially our mothers. Our mother has had a unique relation with us. She has literally made us, and held us inside herself for months. She has nursed, protected, and raised us. She was the first person to love us. At least, that is how it should have been, and how we have always expected it to be. In this relation there was, or ought to have been, loyalty in its purest form—support lasting through time, not for any advantage, nor because of any gift or talent we may have had. Whether we were beautiful or ugly, healthy or ill, intelligent or stupid, our mother loved us—or at least we expected and needed her to do so. It is a need already inherent in our circuitry. We are programed to give and receive loyalty.

We all know that these hopes are betrayed, if not by the mother, then by other people: friends, lovers, spouses, children, and so forth. We know that the world of emotions is in continual change, and that the enthusiasm of today can become the indifference or dislike of tomorrow. In a story taken from Farid al-Din Attar's marvelous poem *The Conference of the Birds*, a beautiful but capricious princess sees a poor young man on the road. He is asleep on a slab of stone by the roadside. The princess takes a fancy to him and orders that he be brought to her palace. Her maidservants take him from the street, bring him to the palace, wash him, massage him with precious oils, dress him in clothes of the finest silk, and finally take him, still overcome by surprise, to the princess. The two of them eat a meal together. For the poor young man, hungry as usual, the food is a benediction. Afterward, they make love and enjoy together a night of ecstasy. At the end, the princess has had enough and, while the man is asleep, orders her maids to take him back to the slab of stone where she had found him. When the poor man wakes up, the heavenly pleasures of the night before are still vivid in his mind. It is like waking from an extraordinary dream to the hard reality of everyday life. The princess has already forgotten him. Or perhaps she never existed. And yet his skin is still fragrant with the royal perfumes.

The story of the princess is meant to symbolize the grace of God. When that grace comes in the form of spiritual enlightenment, it is unexpected, and when it goes away, it leaves us in a state by contrast grim and hard. But it also reminds us of the fickleness in human relations. Loyalty is never guaranteed, disappointment is the rule. In the Age of Distraction, loyalty has become even rarer. And it is for this reason that, when found, it is so precious.

BESIDES THE RELATIONSHIP WITH THE MOTHER, THE place where we are most likely to find loyalty is in friendship. "Hold me in thy heart," Horatio tells Hamlet. This is the phrase that, according to Stuart Miller, who has written a beautiful book on the subject, best defines friendship. To hold a friend in the heart without judgment, without demand—simply to care for this person because we are interested in what he thinks about our ideas and because we know he is ready to listen to and understand us and be on our side. Even though other factors are at play in friendship, its essence is loyalty.

Friendship heals and regenerates. We all know that. And if we need a scientific study to prove it, here it is: Several depressed women were asked, instead of engaging in therapy sessions, to confide in a friend once a week. For most of the women, the depression disappeared with the same rate as in a control group who had weekly therapy sessions. Yet other research has shown the importance of friendship for children's adaptation to school and their academic achievement. Other research has shown the general importance of friendship for our health and well-being.

Hand in hand with loyalty go reliability and faithfulness. They are all qualities allied to constancy and sincerity of affection. In professional fields, we talk of reliability. Here, you do not find the same feelings as in the relationship between children and parents, or between friends. But reliability is nonetheless highly desirable. If I think of the times in my life when I have been more reliable and less reliable, two situations come to mind. One was at the beginning of my career, when I was scheduled to give a five-day workshop for an institute. I was exhausted even before starting, and the day before the workshop I decided to phone and cancel. As no one was there, I left a message on the answering service, washing my hands of the whole thing. I caused considerable trouble, although with my limited professional experience, I did not quite realize it. Even today, if I think of it, despite having abundantly excused myself at the time, I feel uncomfortable.

The moment of greater reliability, instead, was when I had to give a lecture during a big freeze in Florence. The entire town was immobilized by a huge snowstorm. When it snows in Florence, things always come to standstill, but this time it was much worse. The cold was polar, people could hardly leave their homes, public transport was not operating, and you could not drive on the streets. I decided to go anyway—on foot, in the snow—and it took me two hours to get there. I gave the lecture to handful of people. When I recall it, I am glad I did. I know I did the right thing, and I like myself for doing it.

That is loyalty: first and foremost, it is loyalty to ourselves. Reliability is above all internal coherence. Faithfulness is loyalty to your own feelings. When we are loyal and reliable, we feel a fundamental integrity that gives us a sense of well-being. When we are disloyal or unreliable, we might gain some immediate advantage but sooner or later we will feel fragmented and guilty. We have seen in earlier chapters that in not forgiving, we may suffer greater ill-health, and in speaking falsehood, we will feel stress. Just so, in not keeping promises, in betraying someone, in taking advantage of a relationship, we assume an attitude that, even more than harming another, will harm us.

Loyalty is a value so strong that if we do not respect it, we risk coming to an impasse; all our plans, discoveries, and insights risk turning to banality or downright suffering. In a traditional Hasidic story, two young men are the best of friends. One of them grows ill and knows that death is near. While his friend despairs, he accepts death with serenity. Taking the other's hand, he says to the friend, "You cannot fight death. But do not be afraid, I will come back to affirm our friendship, to speak to you of my journey, to tell you I love you. I will not leave you." Then the young man dies. The gates of heaven open before him, and one after another, great truths are revealed to him. He understands the meaning of life and reaches the place where space and time, with their cruel constraints, no longer exist. He becomes one with Eternity. But at one point he realizes that something has gone wrong. He finds himself suddenly imprisoned again in space and time. He feels oppressed but cannot understand why. And then he is told this difficulty has occurred because he had not kept his promise to his friend, did not return to speak of his journey. He can do it now, by speaking through his friend's dreams. But in the meantime, his friend (for whom a long time has passed) has felt abandoned and has lost faith. He has become cynical, does not believe anymore in his dreams. The dead friend can still redeem the situation. He has to climb to the highest level, the

Temple of Truth, then return to his friend. He tells him about the marvels he has seen, gives him the kiss of Paradise. The friend receives this blessing, affirms life, and finds his faith again.

How is it that a friend's loyalty gives us strength and hope? Because in this quality we see a person's true measure. When we show loyalty in hard circumstances, we show how much we care, we show the stuff we are made of. It is easy to be loyal and faithful to someone when all is well. But if we remain loyal when the person is unpleasant or boring, when we gain no advantage in seeing her, when we have more interesting or important matters to attend to, that is where our substance shows. That is where we are seen for what we are.

Sometimes we see loyalty straightaway, in the beauty of a face, in an attitude or a word. In other cases, only time will tell. Always, loyalty gives substance and strength to kindness. In a world so often distracted and careless, this is a priceless value.

GRATITUDE

The Easiest Way to Be Happy

Once upon a time there was a man who hated his job.

He was a stonemason and he had to work all day long for a miserable salary. "What an awful way to live," he thought. "Oh! If only I could be rich and loaf all day!" His wish grew so intense that in the end it came true. The stonemason heard a voice saying, "You are what you want to be." He became rich and could immediately have anything he had always wanted: a beautiful house, delicious food, great entertainment.

He was happy until one day he saw a king pass by with his procession, and he thought, "He is more powerful than I. How I would like to be in his shoes!" Once again he heard the voice, and, as if by magic, he became king. He had become the most powerful man in the world. What a thrill is power! All obeyed him, all feared him. He was happy for a while, but it did not last. Bit by bit, a wicked dissatisfaction took hold of him. "I want more," he thought. "I want, I want, I want." He saw the sun in the sky and thought, "The sun is even more powerful than I. I want to be the sun!"

He became the sun, big, strong, and bright. He ruled earth and sky. Nothing could exist without him. What happiness! And what importance! But then he noticed that beneath him the clouds prevented him from seeing the landscape. They were light and mobile. Instead of being a fixed shape in the sky, they could take an infinite variety of forms, and at sunset they flushed with the most striking colors. They had no cares and were free. How enviable.

His envy did not last long. Once more he heard the voice, "You are what you want to be." And at once he was a cloud. It was pleasant to be suspended in the air, mobile and fluffy. He enjoyed himself taking different shapes, now thick and opaque, now rich and white, now as fine as embroidery. But sooner or later the cloud condensed into raindrops and struck a rock of granite.

What an impact! The rock had been there for millennia—hard and solid. And now the little drops of water burst on the granite and flowed onto the earth, where they were absorbed to disappear forever. "How wonderful to be a rock," he thought.

Instantly he became a rock. For some time, he enjoyed his life as a rock. At last he had found stability. Now he felt secure. "After all, it is security and solidity I am seeking, and no one is going to move me from here," he thought. The raindrops struck the rock and trickled down its sides. It was a pleasant massage, a gift. The sun caressed and warmed him with its rays—how beautiful. The wind refreshed him. The stars watched over him. He had attained completeness.

Well, not yet. One day, he saw a figure approaching on the horizon. It was a man, slightly bent and with a large hammer—a stonemason, who began striking the hammer against him. Worse than pain, he felt dismay. The stonemason was even stronger than he and could decide his destiny. "How I wish I could be a stonemason," he thought.

Thus the stonemason became once again a stonemason. After

being everything he wanted to be, he became again what he had always been. But this time he was happy. Cutting stones had become an art, the sound of the hammer was music, the fatigue at the end of the day brought the satisfaction of a job well done. And that night in his sleep, he had a wonderful vision of the cathedral his stones were helping to build. It seemed to him that there was nothing better to be than what he was. It was a magnificent revelation he knew would never leave him. It was gratitude.

The stonemason in this story makes a basic change. From restless dissatisfaction—"I want this, I want that"—to gratitude—"I am thankful for what I have." In the first state, there is duality because we want what we do not have. We ask, feeling that we have the right. Sometimes we ask with passion, even arrogance, and when we have it, we desire something else. Other people are competition: we view them suspiciously.

In the second state, we are one with what we are given. We feel that this is the moment we have always been waiting for. This makes life worth living. Other people are our friends, not opponents. We feel every cell of our body saying thanks. William Blake said it so well: "Gratefulness is heaven itself."

We are struck by the emotional intensity of gratitude, and by its purity. But emotion is merely the most obvious aspect of gratitude. This is first of all an attitude of the mind. It is based on recognizing the value of what life offers us. That which before did not have value now has value, and this realization frees our emotions.

If we recognize the value of what we have, we feel rich and fortunate. If we do not recognize it, we feel poor and unhappy. It is common to feel like the stonemason in his first attitude: Discontent gnaws at us; grumbling is the undertone to our whole day. According to some psychologists, depression is caused not by what happens to us but by what we tell ourselves day after day—our own inner monologue. If we continually criticize ourselves and others, find only what is wrong, and feel sorry for ourselves, we will surely be unhappy.

The ability to see value even in humble, unremarkable situations is essential to our happiness, or at least to our well-being. Some people seem to have had everything in life but are not content because they do not see the value of what they have, and concentrate on what they still would like, or on what makes them unhappy. Others, instead, maybe less fortunate, appreciate simple things that many of us take for granted—good health, a fine day, a smile.

The possibility of feeling grateful is open to us in every moment of our life. And yet we often miss this opportunity. That happens because to be grateful we have to be without defenses—a risky predicament. We have to renounce our pride in order to recognize that our happiness depends on someone else. Many people do not like to feel they are dependent. I knew a man who was unable to receive presents. Whenever anyone gave him something, a book or a tie, he would leave it behind, as if afraid of being in debt. It stopped him not only from enjoying the book or the tie, but also from opening to another person.

To be grateful is to let ourselves be known. I remember when, some years ago, an Australian friend who was traveling in Europe came to visit my wife and me. We decided to take her to Vinci and spend some time at the birthplace of Leonardo—a glorious September afternoon among olive trees and the remembrance of a genius. At the end of the outing, our friend said goodbye to us with the simple words "Thank you." In that moment I saw in her eyes pure gratitude. We had not made any special effort—it had been a pleasure. She had enjoyed the visit and given it much value. In the years to come, we met her several times, but now whenever I think of her,

I remember that day, that moment of gratitude. Why? When we are grateful, all our defenses drop and we show ourselves for who we are. In that moment I had seen her essence.

GRATITUDE IS BY DEFINITION ANTIHEROIC. IT DOES NOT depend on courage or strength or talent. It is based on our incompleteness. If we do not hide it from ourselves, we can receive the goodness that life offers us and we can be grateful. The great sense of relief that comes with gratitude derives from the recognition that we cannot manage alone, that we do not have to strive to be a superman or superwoman, and that even if we are not *so* brilliant, we are fine as we are.

But wait a minute. Do I have to be grateful to absolutely everybody—to a neighbor who plays rock music at full volume late at night, to the policeman who fines me unjustly, or to whoever spat out the chewing gum I just stepped in? And am I supposed to be grateful (here we reach the heart of the matter) if my son takes hard drugs, or my business is ruined, or a dear one is afflicted with an incurable illness? How are we to take the evils accompanying us throughout our lives? How are we to cope with the tragedies that are far away for many of us yet so terribly close as to never leave us— abused children, tortured political prisoners, endless wars, hunger and thirst, the rampant suffering and disgrace of the planet?

Gratefulness does not mean enjoying one's own pleasures while forgetting about other people. True gratitude is born only where solidarity and the awareness of evil are present—otherwise it is not gratitude at all but consumerism and false or superficial optimism. Strange but true: If everything always went smoothly, we would take for granted all that was beautiful and would not fully appreciate the gifts of life. We would be like spoiled kids who have received so many presents, they have grown bored. Indeed, sometimes it is the dramas of life that open us to gratitude.

It's a paradox: When we have been sick, we appreciate health; when we make up after a fight, we rediscover friendship; when we are close to death, we love life. This also happens in the wider dimension. An online study based on 4,817 responses asked subjects to rate their own personalities. Compare the responses before September 11 and two months after, and you find an increase in seven aspects: gratitude, hope, kindness, leadership, love, spirituality, and group collaboration. Ten months after the terrorist attack, the increase still held, but less than before. Let's not count on it, nor wish it on anyone, but it seems that sometimes a shock evokes our dormant resources.

Fortunately, there are easier roads to gratitude. We just have to look closer. In the hidden folds of our life, we can find forgotten or unsuspected treasures, which we have not appreciated for want of time or attention. They are the gifts of life, some apparently banal, some special. If we are distracted, we miss them; if we notice them, we are happier.

My son Emilio spends his savings on a model airplane kit. When he opens the box, he has an unpleasant surprise—the box is magnificent, but the contents are disappointing. The materials are of poor quality, the instructions unclear, the whole kit seems to be a rip-off. Emilio is upset. I can understand him: He is like me—bad quality infuriates him. I do not know what to do. I would like to console him. Should I offer him the money he has spent? Or buy him some better model airplanes? Doubtful, I stay out of it. Emilio abandons the project. A few days later, his friend Andrea happens to be at our home and see the airplanes. "Wow! What beautiful planes! Fabulous colors! Boy, are you lucky! How come you haven't assembled them yet?" I study Emilio's face. I see the little wheels in his brain turning: his GQ (gratitude quotient) is rising exponentially. The two boys set to work. It matters little that the quality is mediocre, and they do without the instructions altogether. Minutes later, the kids are in the garden flying them. What was before a rip-off has become a treasure. Couldn't we do the same with our own little planes?

We can. And if we do, we will find that gratefulness boosts our health and our efficiency. A recent study looked at three groups of subjects. The first had to note down only irritations and frustrations in the course of a week; the second had to note all significant events; the third had to note up to five items for which to be grateful in their lives. This went on every week for ten weeks. Subjects were distributed at random in the three groups. At the end, the subjects who had noted reasons to be grateful were the ones who felt best about their lives in general, had more optimistic expectations of the future, felt best physically, and believed themselves to have made most progress toward their goals. Gratitude seems to be a factor not only in our happiness, but also in our health and efficiency.

This finding should not surprise us. People who feel gratitude acknowledge inner richness and affirm a relationship. This is the basis of good health. Whenever one of my psychotherapy clients feels gratitude, I know she is healed. For me, it is the single most certain criterion for knowing how well a person is. It shows that her channels of communication are open, that she neither overestimates herself (as she knows she needs others) nor underestimates herself (as she knows she deserves what she receives). It means that she is capable of seeing the value in her actual situation. She can appreciate what is good in her life. What more does anyone want?

To be kind without being grateful is dangerous, perhaps impossible. People who do not know how to receive, and do not feel thankful for what they have been given, are in trouble when they try to be kind. They think they are being great benefactors and everyone should be indebted to them. Maybe they even remind others of their own good deeds, expecting gratitude. They become condescending. Also, it is harder for them to appreciate subtle, seemingly insignificant aspects—for example, a smile, half an hour in someone's company, a witty remark. They value only concrete and measurable gifts, such as a watch or a fountain pen. But kindness does not fit onto a balance sheet.

Gratefulness is easily forgotten, but also easily evoked. Here is an interesting experiment: Think of all the people in your life to whom you can be grateful—all the main ones, that is. The hard part of this experiment is that the people to whom we may feel gratitude are often those toward whom we also feel resentment, for instance our parents. Resentment usually obscures gratitude, but the skill in this experiment is in bracketing our reproaches, however big, and in concentrating on good aspects, however small.

Let us think, then, about the people in our life to whom we are grateful. There are plenty of people—many more than we believe—who perhaps have done us good, even though we may not have fully acknowledged it: parents, friends, teachers, lovers, and in general all who have made our life a lot or even a little better, like the postman who delivers our mail every day, or the taxi driver who tells us a good joke.

If we give it some thought, we will find much more than we may anticipate because life is made of big and small favors, not only of rudeness and arrogance. True, each one of us carries the wounds of injustice and outrage. We know this only too well. What we forget, because it is so obvious, is that even the lives of those who consider themselves most unfortunate and alone are interwoven with others and could not exist without their support.

If I think of everyone in my life to whom I can feel grateful, an interesting thing happens. Bit by bit I realize that all I have has come to me from others. From my parents I have had wonderful support. My teachers have given me essential instruments for my work, ideas, and inspiration. My friends have helped me feel good about myself. Colleagues have taught me tricks of the trade. Other people have opened me to entire worlds whose existence I scarcely suspected, or have taught me the importance of caring for others. My wife and my children have given me love and a wealth of surprises. And this is just the beginning. Gradually, as I continue, I realize all that I have—possessions, abilities, character traits, ideas—comes from others or has been evoked by the presence of others.

Little by little, I recognize that each brick of my house has been given by someone—and my own bricks, in turn, have contributed to many other houses. So, how do I feel? Is my pride hurt, my self-sufficiency threatened, am I in everyone's debt? Not at all. Rather, my image of myself and others changes. We have been educated to think we are all individuals with well-defined boundaries, and we need to roll up our sleeves and get cracking in order to improve ourselves and produce something worthwhile. This is Western culture. Some even believe they owe nothing to anyone. This is a billiard ball picture of ourselves: separate individuals surrounded by other separate individuals.

But this image is false. We are more like cells with a permeable membrane, living by continuous exchange and depending on other cells for our life. Gratitude is a realistic view of what we are. Credit and debit belong to the accountancy and billiard ball mentality. Instead, here the exchange is continuous and determines what we are and how we live. If we begin to think in this way, we can feel more relaxed. Gratitude is no longer an exceptional event but a basic feeling. And while ingratitude means coldness and distance, gratitude is warmth, openness, intimacy. Life becomes much easier. We are no longer anxious to prove how clever we are. And we stop whining and complaining. We do not have to undertake bloody battles nor attempt impossible victories. We discover that happiness is already here. It already exists, unsuspected. Right in front of our eyes.

SERVICE

A Wonderful Opportunity

I am waiting for my cappuccino, standing at the bar. Next to me, an attractive young woman with red hair and freckles, clearly a foreigner, has also ordered a cappuccino. Serving at the bar is a young man with curly dark hair. With an air of nonchalance, he places her cup down. It has lovely froth, with a perfect creamy heart in the middle. I peek at her reaction and notice her surprise. She is not used to receiving a heart for breakfast. The barman says nothing, does not even look at her. Then my cappuccino arrives—no heart, just a banal cappuccino like any other. Simply a drink, no love message.

I must admit a slight feeling of envy for those two. But that is not the point. What *is* important lies in their interior, secret world. I do not know the sequel to this episode and can only guess. The more cynical hypothesis is that the barman does the same trick many times a day, whenever a good-looking girl comes along, and that sooner or later he scores with one of them. And that the redhead, accustomed to flattery, makes nothing much of it. But I do not really

THE POWER OF KINDNESS

believe it went like that. I prefer to think that the woman left the bar and walked the tourist circuit of the town, often so anonymous and cold to its teeming visitors, in a lighthearted mood. Perhaps that day she took in more of the town's beauty and felt happier. And all because, in one of its infinite possibilities and assuming the improbable form of a cappuccino, the spirit of love had reached her.

Perhaps the woman with the red hair will remember this small episode for many years. Because when someone, in his own way, is kind to us, it is likely we will remember it for a long time, maybe forever. For instance, when I was a child, my mother and my aunt took my sister and me on a journey across the United States. In those days, a trip like that was rare. America was an unfamiliar continent, perhaps even a little dangerous (or so we felt) for someone traveling there for the first time, and not knowing the language well. We crossed the country by rail and had to change trains in Chicago. When we arrived there, we realized not only that the trains belonged to two different companies, but also that the arrival of the one and the departure of the next were at two different stations. We had just one hour for changing trains in a place where everything was unfamiliar.

This became an extraordinary adventure (we made it just in time), and the part that will remain forever impressed in my memory took place in a creaky, wobbly elevator, so slow its descent seemed endless. There we were, two women and two children, all four of us lost and scared. I remember that several people spoke to us, made us feel welcome, and told us where to go and what to do. Some talked to my sister and me, and one person even gave her a rag doll, pulled out from who knows where. That trip in the creaky elevator was in another dimension, far from timetables and from hurry, where we met people who gave us serenity. Many years later, I still recall it with gratitude.

What interests me most in stories such as these, and in so many others you and I can recall, is the fantastic variety of ways we all have for making another human being feel better. Let us look at a few examples:

- A friend makes a joke that lifts your spirits.
- You need time and tranquillity; a kind soul offers to look after your children, tidy your house, and prepare dinner.
- You have a terrible toothache, and a dentist fixes the problem quickly and painlessly.
- Someone listens to you and understands you fully; you feel at peace with yourself.
- A teacher or therapist or spiritual guide stimulates in you capabilities you never knew you had.
- A book opens you to new perspectives.
- At a concert, the music is so beautiful it moves and transforms you.

And so on. There are infinite ways, implicit or explicit, microscopic or gigantic, episodic or lasting, superficial or substantial, of bringing into the life of another person some benefit, relief, cheerfulness, hope, well-being, intellectual or spiritual growth, ecstasy. This kind of relationship is no angelic exception in a sordid world of selfish and warring individuals. It is, on the contrary, a normal event, often a part of our everyday interactions, at the base of kindness. It is service.

Happily, service is also in the little things, the tiniest ones: to hold the door open for someone, to give warm appreciation, to offer your seat on the bus. A Hebrew story tells of Reb Nachum, a selfish businessman who thinks only of making money and swindling others. One night, on his way home in a carriage, he sees by the roadside a poor farmer whose cart has wound up with its wheels in the mud. The farmer is pushing, but by himself he cannot get the cart back on the road. He is dressed in his very best for the Sabbath. But he is exhausted and distressed because he cannot move his cart. Reb Nachum gets out of the carriage and helps the farmer push. With the two of them, it is easy work and the problem is resolved. As they are saying goodbye, Reb Nachum notices a bit of mud on the farmer's clothes, and almost without thinking, he removes it with a flick of his hand. "Now you are ready for the Sabbath feast," he says and leaves. He goes back to his normal life.

Many years later, Reb Nachum dies and arrives at God's judgment, the accusing angel on one side, the defending angel on the other. The accusing angel examines his life and finds a lot of material. Reb Nachum has devoted himself only to amassing wealth, never to the care of his wife and family; he had no friends, did not help the community, committed dishonest acts, and abused his power. The angel puts it all on the accusing side of the scales, and the balance weighs heavily to that side. The angel of mercy doesn't know what to do. He looks over and over at Reb Nachum's life, finding nothing good: not a kind word, no act of solidarity. Suddenly, he sees the one kind act of moving the cart. In desperation, he takes the whole cart and throws it on the scales. The balance swings to and fro, for a moment seeming to stay in equilibrium, then weighing once more toward the accusing side. The angel does not know what more to do, then at last sees the bit of mud Reb Nachum had brushed off the farmer's clothes: a tiny forgotten act of kindness. So the angel takes the little lump of mud and throws that too on the defense side of the scales. Miracle: the balance shifts. Reb Nachum is saved. You never know: a size *small* service can yield results *extra large*.

It is easy to think of service as sacrifice, because it takes our time and energy. But often it is just the opposite. Service is advantageous to those who do it, not only to those who receive it. The world of business is finding this by way of systematic study and scientific rigor: An increasing amount of research confirms the obvious fact that service is good business. Treating clients well raises the probability that they will like you and come back. The reverse is equally true: How often have we had to wait for ages at a restaurant before being served, or been treated with a couldn't-care-less attitude by a shop assistant, or bought an item we thought was of good quality, only to find out it was a piece of junk? A firm has everything to gain by respecting clients. Its task is to reduce the "terrorists": unsatisfied customers who, besides not coming back, spread the bad word about that firm. It turns out that unsatisfied clients speak of a negative experience to nineteen people on average. The other task is to increase the number of "apostles": satisfied clients who not only come back, but also do free advertising. It seems that the factors most efficacious in making clients come back are:

- Keeping one's word: delivering the goods
- Being flexible with unusual requests
- Helping those who need help
- Being friendly and warm: putting the client at ease
- Being honest: never lying
- Showing kindness: treating clients with courtesy and respect

Of course, treating clients well so that they come back is not disinterested kindness—it is just knowing how to do good business. Yet I am convinced that (a) interested kindness is better than disinterested rudeness; and (b) those who pretend to be kind find so many advantages in this attitude that they often end up being kind for real.

Like all good things, however, service also comes with a multitude of dangers and gremlins. The most common one is charging—attaching a price to the good that is done—and then presenting the bill, even years later. In my work as psychotherapist, as I listen to clients talk about their parents, one grievance comes up more than any other. And what is it? Pressure? Mistreatment? Negligence? Humiliation? Threat? These certainly abound. But the most common complaint is leveled at parents who remind their children of all that they have done for them. To hear the list of favors, sacrifices, and efforts committed on their behalf is an intolerable ordeal. Nonetheless, it is natural that parents want their children not to take all their work for granted. The job of a parent is hard, unacknowledged, and unpaid, and in the end the kids are often not even grateful for it. How is it, then, that their reaction is so strong? Because once upon a time their service was disinterested, but now it has become an instrument for retort. In this way, all the goodness of the past is eliminated with one blow. It works like this: Again and again you receive what you believe is an act of gratuitous kindness, and then later, with an unexpected, posthumous rereading, you find out that you have to pay. It is like making love passionately, then finding out that it was a professional performance and here is the bill. A spontaneous gift has become an item in a budget: Its original beauty has suddenly vanished.

Let us think of the opposite situation: Someone helps you, and far from reminding you of it, she does not even mention the good she has done, perhaps because she is already busy doing more good somewhere else. This person does not take herself too seriously. She is not heavy and solemn, and may even be humorous. And if no one points out to you the favor you have received, you have a greater capacity to enjoy it since you do not feel in debt or guilty or in need of defending yourself. Perhaps you will never notice what—through effort, devotion, possibly even risk—has been done for you. Too bad. But no one grabs you by the collar asking for payment. You have more space inside, and therefore you will be more likely one day, maybe in the distant future, to suddenly realize the goodness you were given and feel arising in you a spontaneous feeling of gratitude.

Another problem: Transforming service, which in essence is the forgetting of self, into an opportunity for showing how clever we are. Placing ourselves at the center, and making gratitude to us a duty. It makes others feel like being in one of those houses where the walls are covered with diplomas and certificates, photographs of the owner in the company of famous people, special edition books to show off high culture, and generally all that could celebrate the greatness and importance of the host. You are just about forced to admire. But do you feel uplifted, enriched, or nourished? No way.

In any case, the metaphor of the house is appropriate for representing relationships. Imagine now that the house, rather than being pretentious and self-centered, is a sinister and inhospitable place. Watch out! There's a rusty nail sticking out, and a loose floorboard. You could hurt yourself. The paintings on the wall are anguish-inducing. Some rooms are off limits. The chairs are uncomfortable. Or imagine a depressing house, where you read dejection everywhere—dust, disorder, and dismay are all over the place.

Then there are also happy homes where the atmosphere is full of warmth and you feel at ease the moment you enter. You are offered food and drink, and you find all kinds of interesting stimuli everywhere—books, pictures, statuettes. You feel welcome.

Homes are like people, and service is not just what you do, but what you are. Sometimes certain people, by their mere presence, make us feel better, more in contact with ourselves, happier. At other times, they have an equally good but more intellectual effect. When I was at high school, I had a great philosophy teacher. He barely followed the curriculum. He would reproach those who learned their work by rote and praised anyone coming up with an original thought. Books and journals with the capacity to move and to transform were far more interesting to him than compulsory texts. He spoke of current events, politics, contemporary thought, or his personal history as a freedom fighter. During his classes, everyone's attention was always alive.

These lessons had an extraordinary effect on me. They taught me that I could think with my own head. It was like discovering that till then I had existed in a small attic of a huge house, but that in fact the entire house was mine and now I could go into all the rooms. While before I would follow thoughts that were served to me like dinner on the table, almost from one day to the next I discovered in myself the capacity to think.

This novelty put me in conflict with some authorities, but it was a wonderful gift. And it all happened not so much because of any particular piece of teaching, but through the intellectual vitality the professor was able to transmit. During World War II, he had participated in the Italian Resistenza, fighting against the Fascists and the Nazis. His loathing of any form of authoritarianism and dictatorship, his passion for liberty and freedom of thought for which he had risked his life more than once, had so become part of his being that perhaps even without realizing it, he communicated these values and infected everyone with them.

Here we see a basic fact: We transmit what we are, and we are what we have worked to become. The philosophy professor transmitted his passion for liberty and his intellectual vitality because he had cultivated them for many years, and because he had been ready to risk his life to save and honor these values. Had they been less important for him, he would not have been able to convey them.

Let us look at this process step by step:

1. At any moment of our lives, requests for help and occasions for service all about us abound. We have only to look. The kids need help with homework, a passerby needs directions to the station, the endangered natural environment is crying out in pain, or an old person, forgotten by everybody, is dying.

2. If we do not respond to these requests, we will probably feel ill at ease. If we do respond, we will have to develop the ability to satisfy them. We need patience to help the children, we need the appropriate knowledge to help nature, we have to be able to find the old person who is dying alone. Or we simply need to know the way to the station.

3. The process for discovering and developing abilities and knowledge for doing useful work takes a lifetime and arouses in us unsuspected potential. It involves not only knowing the way to the station, but also the ability to say it clearly and the kindness to stop and explain, even when in a hurry and sacrificing precious time. We are all offering the products of our work. If I have to give a lecture that is to be useful in some way to those who hear it, I first have to study and research my subject, ask myself what would strike my audience as interesting, produce some original thoughts on the matter. I also have to overcome the anxiety of speaking in public, develop the capacity to enter into a relationship with my listeners, and create a pleasant and stimulating atmosphere.

If, say, I am working with the dying, I have to have faced to some extent my own anxieties about death, I have to learn to be present even when I feel like running away, accept the most unpleasant aspects of sickness; I have to be at ease with intimacy; and so on. This whole process changes me, enriches me, and places me more in contact with all my faculties.

4. To offer something useful to someone can reward us personally. We may receive gratitude and admiration, and go home satis-

fied. But very often it does not happen like that. Millions of parents have done a lot for their children, but the children grow up and mistreat or forget them. Doctors, teachers, nurses, tradesmen have devoted their lives to serving a litigious, demanding public, which takes their service and spirit of sacrifice for granted. A cook might take hours to prepare a delicious dinner, but the customers devour it in minutes and do not even pay him a compliment. Many volunteer workers regularly face waiting, boredom, ingratitude, and even hostility.

This is the decisive stage of service, because it is here that we are put to the test. If our true goal is to gain admiration and recognition, show how good we are, or collect brownie points, sooner or later we will give up. If instead the motivation is to help someone heal, feel better, find herself, know what to do and make progress in her growth, then we will continue. Service helps us purify our own motivation, become disinterested, and therefore freer.

This is the sequence. Now, I think one fact is evident: Service helps not only the receiver, but also the server. Whoever offers service must improve himself in order to do what has to be done, must think about others rather than only about himself. He learns. He finds value in what he does. Thus his self-esteem grows, and he is able to find meaning in his life. He enters into relation with another human being. And if, inevitably, he meets frustration, failure, or ingratitude, his motivation is put to the test and he has the possibility of emerging stronger for it.

Serving others brings about the best in ourselves. This is apparent even in small episodes of everyday life. I once knew by sight a person in my neighborhood who had a bad reputation. He was a bulky man of about thirty, with an apelike appearance. He would walk around grim-faced, scaring people by his very demeanor. I had heard he had been in trouble with the law. People would steer clear of him, eye him suspiciously. One day when I was in a hurry for an appointment, my tire blew just as I was leaving. I started to use the jack but found it was faulty. As I dithered on the roadside, my anxiety rose, and who should drive by but this man. He offered to help, and after a moment of hesitation, I accepted. In no time at all, he changed my tire. What struck me then was how he had completely changed: In a few seconds, an asocial, possibly dangerous creature had become a smiling example of human kindness. Very little was necessary to bring out the best in him, the best that perhaps no one knew, perhaps not even he. And this happened because he felt he could be useful.

There are many studies that show the positive effects altruistic service has on the server. Altruistic service is beneficial to cardiac patients, for instance, because it fights two big dangers: depression and isolation. Among veterans of the Vietnam War, it was found that those with an altruistic disposition were less subject to post-traumatic stress disorder, a condition that can affect a patient for years. In another study, volunteers for a risky biomedical study still had greater self-esteem twenty years after the study had finished. In yet another research on volunteer work, six aspects of personal well-being were measured: happiness, satisfaction in life, self-esteem, sense of being able to control one's own life, physical health, and absence of depression. All had increased in subjects who had done volunteer work.

But the most important effect goes way beyond the tangible benefits and statistical data. It is a profound change that occurs in us. What emerges is the basic attitude of being open and sensitive to the needs and problems of others and thus ready to do something to help, in both small and big matters. For example, one day when I was still living in town, the doorbell rang and when I opened the door, an elderly man told me, "You left your headlights on." "Thank you, but how did you know it was my car, and that I live here?" It turned out he had looked inside the car, seen a letter on the car seat with my name and address on it. I can imagine this scenario for myself: I am passing by and I see a parked car with the lights on. Do I keep going, thinking I am glad it did not happen to me? Or do I, like this man, go to the trouble of doing something about it? Realizing that in this moment life has brought me an opportunity, I can choose to act. Tomorrow another opportunity will arise: a friend will be feeling lonely, there'll be dinner to cook, a scared child to comfort. I will be ready.

It is a basic attitude in which, to some extent, we transcend ourselves. Our needs, worries, gripes are temporarily put to one side. We forget them for a while because there is work to be done elsewhere. And it is exactly this capacity of self-transcendence that helps us, because it frees us from the prison of our own ego. We are usually shut in with everything that makes us hope and suffer: the prison of our ego. In the end, however interesting it might be, it will limit and oppress us. If it is full of nightmares and terrible memories, we will go mad. Then we find a key to get out: looking after others, being interested in their predicament, making contact. And that is the key to our own freedom.

But there are still more difficulties. Sometimes service runs into the belief that all we can possibly do is useless, that we live in a world full of injustice, abuse of power, sickness, unhappiness of such huge dimensions that whatever we do will only have a fleeting, insignificant effect, or no effect at all. And that, whether we like it or not, we are useless. Sooner or later, service brings us face to face with our ability to influence the lives of others. Are we able to change their lives for the better, or are we impotent to do anything about their predicament?

Maybe we ought to think in another, deeper way, and realize that we live in a world of subtle interactions and unpredictable turns of events. In a story the Buddha told, a parrot wants to save the animals of a forest trapped by a terrible fire. The parrot dives into the river, then flies over the fire beating its wings, hoping the few drops that fall on the fire might put it out. Just so, we are aware that our few drops cannot save the world. The fire grows bigger and bigger. It is a merciless threat. The animals scream in fright. The parrot, covered in soot, is exhausted from its continuous efforts. We too sometimes find ourselves in awful and insoluble situations, problems bigger than we are. The parrot continues, and after some time the gods, so often distracted and indifferent to earthly suffering, are moved by the goodwill and heroism of the parrot. Their tears, falling on the earth, become rain—a benevolent rain that puts out the fire, a miraculous balm that saves the terrified animals. Over the devastating fury of the fire, the dedication of a tiny parrot emerged as winner. It was the triumph of the heart.

JOY

Our Natural State

Is there such a person as an expert in joy? I believe there is, and the greatest one I have known was Roberto Assagioli, the founder of psychosynthesis. He was an expert because he had studied joy, but above all because he embodied joy. When I met Assagioli, he was like an old, thin rabbi with a white beard. He was surrounded by a roomful of books, and on his desk sat a sphere with all the stars in the heavens. He looked like the archetypal wise old man. In the real world, he was a psychiatrist—he had been the first to introduce psychoanalysis to Italy. Psychoanalysis, however, did not satisfy him because it focused too much on pathology. Assagioli was interested in positive qualities such as beauty, love, faith, harmony, peace, and joy. For him, our true essence, more profound than any anguish or desperation we may feel, is a center of consciousness that is free. To find this center gives joy. It is our natural state, the way we were meant to be.

Many of the ideas expressed in this book I learned from Assagioli. He used to keep an archive of notes, with one or more files for each quality. For him these qualities were not abstract concepts but living beings like us. And if qualities are living beings, then it is possible for us to meet them and spend some time in their company. They can infuse us with their particular note, stimulate us, guide and inspire us.

When I first heard about this concept, I was very skeptical. For me, a spiritual quality like serenity or courage was just an idea. Perhaps it was a good idea, or maybe useful only for giving sermons or passing judgment, as for instance: "You must be brave" or "You should calm down." But for Assagioli, entering into contact with a quality was an experience every bit as real as eating an ice cream or going for a walk. It did not take me long to see that all this was part of his life. There was a whole world I did not know, and which our materialistic culture ignores: a world of subtle and subjective perceptions and energy exchanges. I began to see that all of us radiate what we are, that we can radiate conflict and anger, or harmony and serenity. We have a field of energy around us, an "aura" that interacts with those of others. It was for this reason that when Assagioli entered a room, everyone would suddenly be in a good mood.

At first it all seemed to me like a regression to a world of magic and animism. But Assagioli did not mean it that way. He meant that these realities had to be studied as, for example, electromagnetic waves, which, although invisible, can transmit sounds, images, and therefore ideas and emotions, as in the television. So after every meditation, Assagioli would suggest the technique of irradiation, known for centuries as "blessing" in various spiritual traditions. During a meditation, we charge ourselves with new and positive energy. However, if we do not share this energy and just keep it for ourselves, we risk spiritual congestion. It does us good to radiate it to others. All good things must be circulated, not stored. Assagioli used the Buddhist formula: Love to all beings, compassion to all beings, joy to all beings, serenity to all beings.

One day during a meditation with him, with eyes closed, we reached "joy to all beings," and I opened my eyes to look at Assagioli. He was absorbed in meditation, immersed in joy. I do not think I have ever seen a person radiate joy in so evident and intense a way. And yet this was a person who had been persecuted during the war years, who had lost a son, who had been scorned for his innovative ideas. . . . I watched him with scientific curiosity. But I was soon touched by that joy: As I observed it in him, I felt it stirring in myself. With his eyes closed, Assagioli must have felt that I was watching him. He opened his eyes and looked at me. It was an extraordinarily beautiful moment. I realized that two people could meet in joy—a joy in which neither tried to compete, obtain a favor, or prove a point. It was the joy of being.

From that day, without even a mention, it became almost a ritual. Every time I meditated with Assagioli, when we would come to the "joy to all beings" part, we would both open our eyes and meet on that wavelength. It was one of the most precious teachings I have ever received. Since then I have lost and rediscovered joy many times. I do not for a moment believe I can possess it forever, or evoke it at will. Like anyone else, I often move around in the dark byways of sadness and distrust. But something has changed forever. Joy remains both a certainty and a wondrous possibility.

Joy, or at least a happy, optimistic attitude, is at the core of kindness. Imagine receiving an act of kindness performed in a bleak, reluctant mood. For example, someone offers you a lift home, but sulks all the way. Or prepares a meal for you, but reminds you of all that he is doing for you. Or helps you find the keys you have lost, while giving you a lecture on how careless you are. No one would want kindness of that sort, because true kindness is given happily. You cannot be kind unless you are at least a little cheerful.

Yet many people do not think this way. On the contrary, joy is often considered as almost a form of egoism or shallowness. I know a man who does volunteer work for medical emergency. In Florence, there is a long and noble tradition of working for charity. In olden times, charity workers would dress in black, even wear a hood so as not to be recognized. Service is supposed to be anonymous, and we should not give help and comfort in order to receive gratitude or other gains, but purely out of moral duty. So far so good. This man went to the introductory meeting, where he and all the newcomers were asked why they wanted to do this volunteer work. He replied, "For the joy of service." At these words one of the older members, silently frowning, gave him a long, reproachful look.

That look said, "It will not do to enjoy your own altruism. Service must be based on sacrifice." Perhaps the frowning man was not altogether wrong. True altruism goes against the mainstream and might require that we renounce some selfish benefit—rest, comfort, time to ourselves, and the like. However, do you prefer to be helped by someone who is sacrificing himself, or by someone who is happy to be doing it?

No doubt about it: One component of kindness is a happy disposition. And akin to happiness is humor—a capacity to see the contradictions and absurdities of our life and not take ourselves too seriously. Anyone who has this quality is safe from emotional inflation and the dramas of everyday life. Ever since Norman Cousins cured himself from ankylosing spondylitis by watching Marx Brothers videos, research on the healing and stimulating effects of this marvelous quality has flowered. For instance, it has been discovered that humor makes us more creative: Subjects who had just seen a comic film were faster at solving a practical problem than the others. Humor has also been found to have the power to relieve physical pain—and that is no small virtue.

We also know that humor strengthens the immune system, lowers blood pressure, and reduces stress. Quite a result! But it is better to not analyze humor too much, and to talk about it in small doses. A long time ago, I made the mistake of running an entire workshop on humor. It was the most depressing one I have ever given. As Mark Twain said, studying humor is like vivisecting a frog—you end up with a dead frog. Here I should mention a memory I am quite fond of, from the time I met the Zen master Shunryu Suzuki at his Tassajara monastery in California. Our meeting was a single look. Together with a group of other students and disciples, I was in the meditation hall where I had just practiced Zen meditation. Immediately afterward, Suzuki gave a discourse. After sitting cross-legged for two hours, I was aching to move my limbs and go for a walk. Since I happened to be near the door, I was the first to leave. I soon realized that I had violated a strict rule of the monastery: First, the Master leaves, then everyone else. What a blunder! But it was too late. Suzuki, as he walked through the door, passed close by me and gave me a look. His eyes seemed to me those of a furious samurai, as you sometimes see in old Japanese prints. But at the same time (don't ask me how he did it—I am still wondering myself), those eyes were amused at the awkwardness of the beginner. It was as though he were saying, "Do not worry, it's all right." It was the serene, amused humor of the sage who watches the theater of life and knows that the great illusion of samsara is one with the supreme bliss of nirvana.

LET US NOW RETURN TO THE GENERAL TOPIC OF HAPPINESS— a subject a little easier to discuss because although it is just as elusive, it concerns our basic orientation in life. Two theories predominate: The first says happiness comes when pleasure is at a maximum—the "hedonistic theory." The second holds that we are happy when we find meaning, even if it is through effort and frustration—the "eudaimonistic theory," from the Greek *daimon*, our true self. I find the latter theory more convincing. What counts is what we believe in. Joy comes because our life has meaning.

Mihaly Csikszentmihalyi has said that pleasure by itself is not enough for attaining joy. In his studies on flow, or optimal experience, he recorded the states a large number of people were in at various times of the day. When did they feel in a state of grace—when were they *flowing*? For the most part, it was not when they were just relaxing on the beach or eating a gourmet meal, but while their whole being was involved in an activity that required discipline, attention, and passion. They were playing chess, or playing the violin, or reading a philosophy book, or dancing. Whatever it was, it was what gave their life meaning.

But what counts is not only the state of grace. It is also the basic mood with which we meet each day. And here the essential question is: Are we optimists or pessimists? Many studies demonstrate that an optimistic attitude has several benefits for health. Martin Seligman, in his book on this topic, shows that politicians who use optimistic words in their speeches are more likely to win elections, just as optimistic sports people are more likely to succeed. More recently, a wave of new research and the beginning of "positive psychology" has drawn attention to this very subject. Meanwhile, a study conducted at the Mayo Clinic indicated that of 839 individuals tested thirty years earlier, those classified as pessimists had a forty percent greater probability of dying than those classified as optimists. In general, optimism protects the human organism from cardiovascular disease and improves the efficiency of the immune system. In sum, optimists do have a happier time and smaller medical bills.

But we do not need research to know that joy feels great. The question is, how do we go about it? Or at least how can we become a bit more optimistic? I think that it is not too hard (I am optimistic). There are at least two easy steps everyone can take. First, we must analyze ourselves. Without going too deeply, most of us can quickly find several ways in which we stop ourselves from enjoying life: We are perfectionists, perhaps, or we let guilt haunt us, or we take ourselves too seriously, or else we focus on what is going badly in our lives. It is surprising how the act itself of becoming conscious of our self-sabotage is often enough to loosen the grip of these destructive attitudes. After all, we have been seeking happiness all our lives. When the mothers of young babies, instead of smiling at them, put on an impassive face, the babies protest and grow restless. They want the smile, not a stony face. What Assagioli used to say was probably right after all: We were born to be happy.

But then we do our best *not* to be happy. Frequently enough, we discover a fear of being happy. This may seem absurd: Why should we fear that which we most desire? We are afraid of joy and happiness for several reasons. First, because we feel unworthy, as if happiness were only due those who deserved it after years of labor. Furthermore, it appears frivolous: With all the pain in the world, how dare we be happy? Then again we are afraid that if we stop suffering and start enjoying ourselves, others will envy us and we will end by feeling different and isolated. We are also afraid that once we feel true joy, it will not last, and we will have the added unhappiness of knowing what we have lost. Finally, we fear happiness because at its most intense, it is overwhelming: happiness can be so great that we are afraid it will disintegrate us.

The second way for approaching joyfulness is even simpler: asking ourselves what it is that makes us happy, a good question we rarely ask ourselves. It is odd, yet sometimes our lives are changed by a good question. What is it that makes us happy? Enjoying the beauty of nature, spending time with someone we love, doing physical activity, reading a book, playing music, rediscovering solitude: there are many possibilities, some of them very far, but some of them surprisingly at hand. We need only to get on with it. I am convinced that most of us are no more than twenty-four hours from joy—and that joy is in nearly everyone's reach. For others, it might take a little more time.

The main doubt to overcome is that by seeking our own joy, we are somehow subtracting that of others. Actually, selfishness and altruism can be friends, not enemies. If we seek joy, we will be much more positive and open to others. We will be on their side. A multitude of studies shows that if we are happy, we are also more altruistic. Other studies show that if we are altruistic, we are also happier. For instance, those who do some kind of volunteer work are usually happier and more balanced than the average.

Further, we are happier if our relationships with those around us are good. Various research shows that the quality (and not the quantity) of our relations is a source of well-being. It has even been shown that health, vitality, and positive emotion vary in proportion to our feeling in rapport with other people. Precisely those who think of others, take part in their lives, try to alleviate their suffering, and feel linked to them are most likely to be happy and to discover the inestimable treasure of joy.

Egoism and altruism need not be in opposition. We can be truly useful to others if we follow that which enriches and inspires us. This is the starting point if we are to bring kindness into our lives. How can we poison ourselves with bitterness, secretly envy others for being more fortunate than we are, complain that we neither do nor have what we want, cry over what does not go our way, plot revenge . . . and at the same time be kind? First, we have to find out what it is that gives us joy. This is a crucial task for everyone. Then it will be more likely that all will go well: Joy renders our relationships easier, more vital, and beautiful.

The essential point here is transparency of intentions. Whoever succeeds in being kind without ulterior motives is more likely to feel joy than she who does the same but hoping for some benefit. "What's in it for me?" This question ends up distracting us. We worry that we might not really get what we want, that we might be cheated, that our kindness might go unacknowledged and unrewarded. In this way, however, we forget to enjoy ourselves.

In an old Eastern story, God wants to reward a man for his exceptional kindness and purity of intentions. He calls an angel and tells him to go to the man and ask him what he wants: He will have whatever his heart desires. The angel appears before the kind man and gives him the good news. The man replies, "Oh, but I am already happy. I have all that I want." The angel explains that, with God, you just have to be tactful. If He wants to give us a gift, it is best to accept. The kind man then replies, "In this case, I would like all who come in contact with me to feel well. But I want to know nothing about it." From that moment, wherever the kind man happens to be, wilted plants bloom again, sickly animals grow strong, ill people are healed, the unhappy are relieved of their burdens, those who fight make peace, and those beset by problems resolve them. And all this happens without the kind man's knowing—always in his wake, but never in front of his eyes. There is never any pride, nor any expectation. Unknowing and content, the kindly man walks the roads of the world, spreading happiness to everybody.

CONCLUSION

How Kindness Happens

My son Jonathan comes home from school, triumphant. "What did you do today?" I ask him. "We did a cleanup in the public park. We wore special gloves, and we collected old newspapers, plastic straws, empty cans and bottles, orange peels, cigarette butts. A man with a special outfit went before us to take away the syringes. We left the park totally clean."

Maybe some of the parents didn't like the idea. But I tip my hat to those teachers because they gave Jonathan and his classmates the chance to be of service to others, without reward, for the pure pleasure of doing so. They gave them the opportunity to be kind.

This initiative of cleaning public parks and beaches, practiced by various groups all over the world, is the quintessence of kindness—not only because it is disinterested, produces useful results, improves the quality of life, and makes the doers happy, but also because it is an effective response to a need or a problem that is right in front of our eyes. Someone is thirsty and you give her water to drink; someone is feeling disheartened and you lift his spirits; the park is full of rubbish and you clean it.

Opportunities for kindness are all around us. Life collaborates, since all we have to do is see the chances for expressing and cultivating kindness. As when we look at those optical illusions in which, after we have gazed at a chaotic image, we see a coherent one emerge, all we have to do is look around, and instead of seeing a boring routine or a series of pressing duties, we find occasions for being kind. They emerge continually in different forms. We just have to pay a little attention.

IN A STORY BY TOLSTOY, A POOR SHOEMAKER HEARS THE voice of Christ in a dream: "Today I will come to you." Then he wakes up and goes to work. During the day, he meets a young woman who is hungry and he gives her food. An old man passes by feeling cold, and he lets him in to warm himself. Later, he takes care of a child who is having problems with his mother. They are all spontaneous acts for which he need give no thought. At the end of the day, before going to sleep, the shoemaker remembers his dream and thinks that it has not come true, since he did not meet Christ. He then hears a voice. It is the voice of Christ, "My dear friend, did you not recognize me? I was that woman, I was that old man, I was the child and his mother. . . . You met me, and you helped me. I was with you the whole day."

Yes, kindness is before our eyes. The opportunity to put things right or to help someone presents itself every moment, and if we respond accordingly, we affirm the truest feelings and highest values life can give.

Each person is kind in his or her own way. There are those who call a friend who is lonely, and those who explain a lesson to a student in difficulty. Someone will give you fresh lettuce from his vegetable garden, or smile at a child in a crowded waiting room. Others will hold the door open for you when you are laden with parcels, and others still will devote their lives to feeding the hungry.

I know a woman who loves animals. She goes around giving food to stray cats and adopts dogs from the pound, rather than let them die because no one wants them. She allots a room in her apartment to keeping many birds free from cages. One day she took home a squirrel. The squirrel then escaped her hold and hid in a cupboard, but she managed to feed it daily. The squirrel would hide during the day, and at night would run about, sometimes landing on her bed while she slept. Not an easy companion. And yet to have set the squirrel free would have meant its death, since the animal was not adapted to living in the wild. After some time, I asked her if she had resolved the problem. "Yes," she answered. "I thought the squirrel was lonely, so I brought it a mate. Now I have two squirrels roaming about the house." For you and me, this might be a nightmare. For her, it is a passion.

Thus, a photographer goes to an orphanage to take pictures of the children, because a fine photograph makes adoption more likely. An old man goes around leaving toys for children at the door of their homes. I have seen people taking sandwiches and hot drinks to the homeless on cold mornings. Young musicians go to hospices and play music for the elderly. And then many people do nothing out of the ordinary—simply what all of us do: they take their kids to school, go to work, prepare food, answer the phone, sweep the floor. They do it with kindness. Infinite are the ways of being kind. We have to find our unique and most consonant way.

But we can never be kind out of guilt or compulsion. Our task is to discover that which we can do best of all, and which gives satisfaction, maybe even joy. That will be our key. Being kind is the simplest way to become who we really are.

Yet sometimes we don't know who we are. Being kind helps us find out. Virginia Satir compares our self-worth with a pot: What is it that fills the pot? Food, rubbish, nothing at all? And what do *we* contain? Security, good memories, intelligence, fine and positive feelings, or shame, guilt, and rage? What do we have to offer? In being kind, we are faced with this question, and we are led to discover resources we perhaps did not know we had. Yet they are resources humanity has always possessed, because they are precisely the abilities that have enabled us to evolve: the care of others, communication and collaboration, the sense of belonging, sharing, empathy. If we gather these faculties, our self-image becomes more positive and complete. We may not know it, we may have forgotten it, but it's true: *We are already kind.*

Being kind does not only bring us into contact with ourselves. It also focuses us on the well-being of others. We are all connected to one another. In the sky of Indra, the Hindu god, are an infinite number of glittering spheres, each reflecting all the others, and therefore the reflections of the spheres in one another. Like the glittering spheres, we all in some way contain everyone else. And if we look inside ourselves, we see that we do participate and react emotionally to what happens on our planet. Billions of people are suffering, hungry, victims of injustice. How can we coexist with such immense problems?

The way we deal with them qualifies our lives. To take a concrete example, think of how your life has changed since September 11. In how many ways has it touched your thoughts, how you feel while you walk down the street, travel, or put your children to bed? In my work as psychotherapist with groups and individuals, I verify all the time just how much the big planetary happenings enter and affect people's minds. I am thinking in particular of certain painful predicaments that, whether we like it or not, resonate deeply in us:

- Hunger. How can we sit down to eat peacefully knowing that 15 million children die of hunger or malnutrition every year?
- War. Some wars take place in front of the cameras; others, equally cruel, without our knowing. They all leave in their wake the suffering due to hatred, pain, and desire for revenge.
- Injustice. Exploitation of children, women, and men; religious fanaticism, totalitarian regimes; political persecution; torture. The intolerable exists.
- Pollution. We live on a planet that has been ill-treated and violated; we have lost our relationship with Mother Earth, to whom we owe our origin.
- The Waste Land. Many of us have lost contact with our soul and are fleeing toward the chimera of consumerism, or else are lost in the fog of depression.

No one can ignore these difficulties because they touch us every day in many ways. But they are so big that we cannot imagine even scratching their surface by ourselves, except a few exceptional individuals who have the capacity to act and inspire others on a large scale. Yet each of us can *take a stand* internally against such disasters—which implies choosing how we want to be. It happens anyway. We have to coexist with these enormous troubles, and we all take some attitude toward them. Perhaps we ignore them to defend ourselves against the anguish they arouse in us. Perhaps we feel guilt. Perhaps we make social and political commitments.

Being kind is taking a stand. By itself, it might not help: Maybe our kindness will be ineffective. The money we send to alleviate hunger might be unwisely used. Helping an old lady cross the road does not eliminate poverty in a faraway country. And for every plastic bottle we pick up on the beach, another ten will be tossed down tomorrow. Never mind. We have affirmed a principle, a way of being.

Just as important is to realize that microcosm is macrocosm: *Each person is the whole world.* As many mystics and visionaries have pointed out, each individual, in some subtle and mysterious way, embodies all people. If we can bring some relief and well-being to just one person's life, this is already a victory, a silent, humble response to the suffering and pain of the planet. This is the starting point.

The problems of humanity can be resolved only by the participation and initiatives of large numbers of people, and by profound cultural changes. But it is short-sighted to see kindness as a lightweight factor. Not only is kindness capable of saving humanity—it is already saving it. Have you ever asked yourself how come the world, with all its complex structures, hasn't collapsed? It is a miracle that this unimaginably complex system goes on without plunging into total chaos. If every day the postman delivers our letters, and the traffic lights work, and the trains run (more or less) on time, and we are lucky enough to find the food we want, and the newspapers are at the newsstands, and children are not (usually) abandoned in the street, and water flows when we turn the tap, and the light goes on when we press the switch, all this is thanks to the work of countless individuals. To be sure, it is their way of earning a living. But if the world still goes on, it is also thanks to their goodwill, to their wish to help make things work for everyone. It is thanks to their—our—kindness.

From this point of view, kindness and the goodwill of many is a resource, an energy on par with oil, water, wind, nuclear, and solar energy. It would be immensely useful (this is already happening) to pay more attention to it, find ways of evoking it and harnessing it, organize training courses for it, teach it in school, publicize it on TV, use it in ads, turn it into a fashion.

Were that to happen, we would soon not only find that kindness yields immense emotional, physical, and social benefits, that it makes us stronger and abler in the jungle of everyday life. We would realize it is a way to liberation. The Dalai Lama sums it all up this way:

> I have found that the greatest degree of inner tranquillity comes from the development of love and compassion. The more we care for the happiness of others, the greater is our own sense of well-being. Cultivating a close, warm-hearted feeling for others automatically puts the mind at ease. It helps remove whatever fears or insecurities we may have and gives us the strength to cope with any obstacles we encounter. It is the principal source of success in life.

Kindness is a way to free us from the weights and obstacles that imprison us. In a story told by the Indian sage Ramakrishna, a woman visits a friend she has not seen for a long time. When she enters her house, she notices that her friend has many spools of colored thread—a magnificent collection. This multicolored exhibition she finds irresistibly tempting, and when her friend goes for a moment into another room, the woman steals a few spools, hiding them under her arms. But the friend notices and, without accusing her, suggests, "We haven't seen each other for so long. Let's dance together to celebrate!" The woman, embarrassed, cannot refuse, but dances in a rigid way, obliged to hold the spools in place under her arms. The other incites her to free her arms and move them in the dance, but she replies, "I can't. I can only dance this way." Ramakrishna would tell this story to illustrate liberation, which is to stop holding on to our possessions, grasping our roles and ideas, clutching our obsessions. To let ourselves go. When we are kind, we are more concerned with others, therefore less enslaved by our ego and its tyranny; the monsters of anxiety and depression have fewer hooks; the blocks and the encumbrances caused by excessive attention to ourselves disappear.

Strange perhaps, and paradoxical, but true: The most sensible way to further *our own* interests, to find *our own* freedom, and to glimpse *our own* happiness, is often not to pursue these goals directly, but to look after *other* people's interests, to help *other* people be freer from fear and pain, to contribute to *their* happiness. Ultimately, it is all very simple. There is no choice between being kind to others and being kind to ourselves. It is the same thing.

REFERENCES

Introduction

Alberti, A. *Il sé ritrovato.* Florence: Pagnini, 1994.

———. *L'uomo che soffre, l'uomo che cura.* Florence: Pagnini, 1997.

Allen, K., J. Blascovich, and W. B. Mendes. "Cardiovascular Reactivity and the Presence of Pets, Friends, and Spouses: The Truth about Cats and Dogs." *Psychosomatic Medicine,* 64, no. 5 (Sept./Oct. 2002):727–39.

Block, P. *Stewardship: Choosing Service over Self-Interest.* San Francisco: Berret-Koehler, 1993.

Dalla Costa, J. *The Ethical Imperative.* Cambridge, MA: Perseus, 1998.

Dowrick, S. *The Universal Heart.* London: Penguin, 2000.

Fratiglioni, L., H. Wang, K. Ericsson, M. Maytan, and B. Winblad. "Influence of Social Network on Occurrence of Dementia: A Community-based Longitudinal Study." *Lancet,* 355 (2000):1315–19.

Salzberg, S. *Lovingkindness: The Revolutionary Art of Happiness.* Boston: Shambhala, 2002.

Sorokin, P. *The Ways and Power of Love.* Boston: Beacon, 1954.

Tiller, W. A., R. McCraty, and M. Atkinson. "Cardiac Coherence: A New Non-invasive Measure of Autonomic Nervous System Order." *Alternative Therapies in Health and Medicine Health,* 2, no. 1 (Jan. 1996):52–65.

Honesty

Godert, H. W., H. G. Rill, and G. Vossel. "Psychophysiological Differentiation of Deception: The Effects of Electrodermal Lability and Mode of Responding on Skin Conductance and Heart Rate." *International Journal of Psychophysiology,* 40, no. 1 (Feb. 2001):61–75.

Jourard, S. *The Transparent Self.* New York: Van Nostrand, 1971.

Pennebaker, J. W., and C. H. Chew. "Behavioral Inhibition and Electrodermal Activity During Deception." *Journal of Personality and Social Psychology,* 49, no. 5 (Nov. 1985):1427–33.

Weeks, D., and J. James. *Eccentrics.* Weidenfeld & Nicolson: London, 1995.

Warmth

Carton, J. S., and E. R. Carton. "Nonverbal Maternal Warmth and Children's Locus of Control of Reinforcement." *Journal of Nonverbal Behavior,* 22, no. 1 (Spring 1998):77–86.

Carton, J. S., and S. Nowicki. "Origins of Generalized Control Expectancies: Reported Child Stress and Observed Maternal Control and Warmth." *Journal of Social Psychology,* 136, no. 6 (1996):753–60.

Herman, M. A., and S. M. McHale. "Coping with Parental Negativity: Links with Parental Warmth and Child Adjustment." *Journal of Applied Developmental Psychology,* 14 (1993):121–36.

Hill, C. A. "Seeking Emotional Support: The Influence of Affiliative Need and Partner Warmth." *Journal of Personality and Social Psychology,* 60, no. 1:112–21.

Kim, K. "Parental Warmth, Control and Involvement in Schooling in Relation to Korean American Adolescents' Academic Achievement." *Dissertation Abstracts International,* 56, no. 2-A (Aug. 1999):559.

Montagu, A. *Touching: The Human Significance of the Skin.* New York: Harper & Row, 1978.

Ornish, D. *Love and Survival.* New York: HarperCollins, 1998.

Prescott, J. W. "Body Pleasure and the Origins of Violence." *Bulletin of the Atomic Scientists,* Nov. 1975:10–20.

Prodomidis, M., T. Field, R. Arendt, L. Singer, R. Yando, and D. Bendell. "Mothers Touching Newborns: A Comparison of Rooming-in Versus Minimal Contact." *Birth,* 22, no. 4 (Dec. 1995).

Richman, E. R., and L. Rescorla. "Academic Orientation and Warmth in Mothers and Fathers of Preschoolers: Effects of Academic Skills and Self-Perceptions of Competence." *Early Education and Development,* 6, no. 3 (July 1995):197–213.

Tatsumi, K., A. Yoshinori, Y. Yokota, M. Ashikaga, S. Tanaka, and T. Sakai. "Effects of Body Touching on the Elderly." *Journal of International Society of Life Information Science,* 18, no. 1 (March 2000):246–50.

Voelkl, K. "School Warmth, Student Participation, and Achievement." *Journal of Experimental Education,* 63, no. 2:127–38.

Forgiveness

Davidhizar, R. E., and C. R. Laurent. "The Art of Forgiveness." *Hospital Material Management Quarterly,* 21, no. 3 (Feb. 2000):48–53.

Farrow, T. F., Y. Zheng, I. D. Wilkinson, S. A. Spence, J. F. Deakin, N. Tarrier, P. D. Griffiths, and P. W. Woodruff. "Investigating the Functional Anatomy of Empathy and Forgiveness." *Neuroreport,* 12, no. 11 (Aug. 8, 2001): 2433–38.

Mickley, J. R., and K. Cowles. "Ameliorating the Tension: Use of Forgiveness for Healing." *Oncology Nursing Forum,* Jan./Feb. 2001:28.

vanOyen Witvliet, C., T. E. Ludwig, and K. L. Vander Laan. "Granting Forgiveness or Harboring Grudges: Implications for Emotion, Physiology, and Health." *Psychological Science,* 12, no. 2 (Mar. 2001):117–23.

Contact

Arnetz, B. B., T. Theorell, L. Levi, A. Kallner, and P. Eneroth. "An Experimental Study of Social Isolation of Elderly People: Psychoendocrine and Metabolic Effects." *Psychosomatic Medicine,* 45, no. 5 (1983):395–406.

Brummett, B. H., J. C. Barefoot, I. C. Siegler, N. E. Clapp-Channing, B. L.

Lytle, H. B. Bosworth, R. B. Williams, and D. B. Mark. "Characteristics of Socially Isolated Patients with Coronary Artery Disease Who Are at Elevated Risk of Mortality." *Psychosomatic Medicine,* 63 (2001):267–72.

Buber, M. *I and Thou.* New York: Free Press, 1971.

Coben, S., W. J. Doyele, R. Turner, and C. M. Alper. "Sociability and Susceptibility to the Common Cold." *Psychological Science,* 14, no. 5 (Sept. 2003): 389–95.

House, J. S. "Social Isolation Kills, but How and Why?" *Psychosomatic Medicine,* 63 (2001):273–74.

Kawabata, Y. *The Tale of the Bamboo Cutter,* trans. D. Keene. Tokyo: Kodansha International, 1998.

Levi, P. *Se questo è un uomo.* Turin: Einaudi, 1956.

Michelsen, H., and C. Bildt. "Psychosocial Conditions on and off the Job and Psychological Ill Health: Depressive Symptoms, Impaired Psychological Wellbeing, Heavy Consumption of Alcohol." *Occupational and Environmental Medicine,* 60 (2003):489–96.

Roberts, E. R., S. J. Shema, G. A. Kaplan, and W. J. Strawbridge. "Sleep Complaints and Depression in an Aging Cohort: A Prospective Perspective." *American Journal of Psychiatry,* 157 (Jan. 2000):81–88.

Stevens, F. C., R. W. Kaplan, R. W. Ponds, J. P. Diederiks, and J. Jolles. "How Ageing and Social Factors Affect Memory." *Age and Ageing,* 28 (1999): 379–84.

Terrel, F. "Loneliness and Fear of Intimacy Among Adolescents Who Were Taught Not to Trust Strangers During Childhood." *Adolescence,* Winter 2000.

Thorbjornsson, C. O., L. Alfredsson, K. Fredriksson, M. Koster, H. Michelsen, E. Vingard, M. Torgen, and A. Kilbom. "Psychosocial Risk Factors Associated with Low Back Pain: A 24 Year Follow Up Among Women and Men in a Broad Range of Occupations." *Occupational and Environmental Medicine,* 55:84–90.

Zuckerman, D. M., S. V. Kasl, and A. M. Ostfeld. "Psychosocial Predictors of Mortality Among the Elderly Poor: The Role of Religion, Well-being, and

Social Contacts." *American Journal of Epidemiology,* 119, no. 3 (1984): 410–23.

Sense of Belonging

Dolbier, C. "The Development and Validation of the Sense of Support Scale." *Behavioral Medicine,* Winter 2000.

Hagerty, B., and R. A. Williams. "The Effects of Sense of Belonging, Social Support, Conflict, and Loneliness on Depression." *Nursing Research,* 48, no. 4 (July/Aug. 1999):215–19.

Hagerty, B. M., R. A. Williams, J. C. Coyne, and M. R. Early. "Sense of Belonging and Indicators of Social and Psychological Functioning." *Archives of Psychiatric Nursing,* 10, no. 4 (Aug. 1996):235–44.

Hagerty, B. M. K., J. Lynch-Sauer, K. L. Patusky, M. Bouwserna, and P. Collier. "Sense of Belonging: A Vital Mental Health Concept." *Archives of Psychiatric Nursing,* 6, no. 3 (June 1992):172–77.

Hunter, E. "Adolescent Attraction to Cults." *Adolescence,* Fall 1998.

Walsh, A., "Religion and Hypertension: Testing Alternative Explanations Among Immigrants." *Behavioral Medicine,* Fall 1998.

Trust

Barefoot, J. C., K. E. Maynard, J. C. Beckham, B. H. Brummett, K. Hooker, and I. C. Siegler. "Trust, Health and Longevity." *Journal of Behavioral Medicine,* 21, no. 6:517–26.

Hampes, W. P. "The Relationship Between Humor and Trust." *Humor: International Journal of Humor Research,* 12, no. 3 (1999):253–59.

Hyde-Chambers, F. and A. *Tibetan Folk Tales.* Shambhala: Boston, 1981.

Kramer, R. M. "Trust and Distrust in Organizations." *Annual Review of Psychology,* 1999.

Lovejoy, B. H. "Trust in Self, Others and God: Influences on Adult Survivors of Hurricane Iniki." *Dissertation Abstracts International,* 56, no. 2-A (Aug. 1995).

McColl, M. A., J. Bickenbach, J. Johnston, S. Nishihama, M. Schumaker,

K. Smith, M. Smith, and B. Yealland. "Changes in Spiritual Beliefs after Traumatic Disability." *Archives of Physical Medicine and Rehabilitation,* 81, no. 6 (2006):817–23.

Yamagishi, T., M. Kikuchi, and M. Kosugi. "Trust, Gullibility, and Social Intelligence." *Asian Journal of Social Psychology,* 2, no. 1 (Apr. 1999):145–61.

Yunus, M. *Il banchiere dei poveri.* Milan: Feltrinelli, 1998.

Zaheer, A., B. McEvily, and V. Perrone. "Does Trust Matter? Exploring the Effects of Interorganizational and Interpersonal Trust on Performance." *Organization Science,* 9, no. 2 (Mar./Apr. 1998):141–59.

Mindfulness

Cleary, T. *The Spirit of Tao.* Shambhala: Boston, 1991.

Forest, H. *Wisdom Tales from Around the World.* Little Rock, AR: August House, 1996.

Langer, E. J. *Mindfulness.* Cambridge, MA: Persus, 1989.

———. "Mindfulness Research and the Future." *Journal of Social Issues,* Spring 2000.

Sternberg, R. J. "Images of Mindfulness." *Journal of Social Issues,* Spring 2000.

Wiseman, R. *The Luck Factor.* New York: Hyperion, 2003.

Empathy

Bellini, L. M., M. Baime, and J. A. Shea. "Variation in Mood and Empathy During Internship." *Journal of the American Medical Association,* 287, no. 23 (June 19, 2002):3143–46.

Carlozzi, A. F., K. S. Bull, G. T. Eells, and J. D. Hurlburt. "Empathy as Related to Creativity, Dogmatism and Expressiveness." *Journal of Psychology,* 129, no. 4 (July 1995):365–73.

Dalai Lama, and D. Goleman. *Destructive Emotions.* New York: Bantam, 2003.

Goleman, D. *Emotional Intelligence.* New York: Bantam, 1995.

Hojat, M., J. S. Gonnella, S. Mangione, T. J. Nasca, J. J. Veloski, J. B. Erdmann, C. A. Callahan, and M. Magee. "Empathy in Medical Students as Related to Academic Performance, Clinical Competence and Gender." *Medical Education,* 36, no. 6 (June 2002):522–27.

Huxley, L. *You Are Not the Target.* New York: Farrar, Straus, 1963; repr. New York: Metamorphous, 1998.

Kearney, M. *Mortally Wounded.* New York: Touchstone, 1997.

Kohn, A. *The Brighter Side of Human Nature.* New York: Basic Books, 1990.

Krebs, D. "Empathy and Altruism." *Journal of Personality and Social Psychology,* 32, no. 6 (Dec. 1975):1134–46.

Lee, H. S., P. F. Brennan, and B. J. Daly. "Relationship of Empathy to Appraisal, Depression, Life Satisfaction, and Physical Health in Informal Caregivers of Older Adults." *Research in Nursing Health,* 24, no. 1 (Feb. 2001):44–56.

Monteith, M. "Why We Hate." *Psychology Today,* 35, no. 3 (May/June 2002):44.

Salzinger, K. "Psychology on the Front Lines." *Psychology Today,* 35, no. 3 (May/June 2002):34.

Humility

Shah, A. *Tales of Afghanistan.* London: Octagon, 1982.

Weiss, H. M., and P. A. Knight. "The Utility of Humility: Self-Esteem, Information Search, and Problem-Solving Efficiency." *Organizational Behavior & Human Decision Processes,* 25, no. 2 (Apr. 1980):216–23.

Patience

Levine, R. *A Geography of Time.* New York: Basic Books, 1997.

Generosity

Cauley, K., and B. Tyler. "The Relationship of Self-Concept to Pro-Social Behavior in Children." *Early Childhood Research Quarterly,* 4 (1989):51–60.

Gardyn, R. "Generosity and Income—for Americans, Those Who Earn the Least Money Tend to Give Away the Most." *American Demographics,* Dec. 1, 2002.

Kishon-Barash, R., E. Midlarsky, and D. R. Johnson. "Altruism and the Vietnam Veteran: The Relationship of Helping to Symptomatology." *Journal of Traumatic Stress,* 12, no. 4 (Oct. 1999):655–62.

Krause, N., B. Ingersoll-Dayton, J. Liang, and H. Sugisawa. "Religion, Social Support, and Health Among the Japanese Elderly." *Journal of Health and Social Behavior,* 40, no. 4 (Dec. 1999):405–21.

Lamanna, M. A. "Giving and Getting: Altruism and Exchange in Transplantation." *Journal of Medical Humanities,* 18, no. 3 (1997):169–92.

Piliavin, J. A., and H. Charng. "Altruism: A Review of Recent Theory and Research." *Annual Review of Sociology,* 16 (1990):27–65.

Renwick Monroe, K. *The Heart of Altruism.* Princeton, NJ: Princeton University Press, 1990.

Russell, G. W., and R. K. Mentzel. "Sympathy and Altruism in Response to Disasters." *Journal of Social Psychology,* 130, no. 3:309–17.

Seelig, B. J., and W. H. Dobelle. "Altruism and the Volunteer: Psychological Benefits from Participating as a Research Subject." *ASAIO Journal,* 47, no. 1 (Jan./Feb. 2001):3–5.

Sesardic, N. "Recent Work on Human Altruism and Evolution." *Ethics.* 106 (Oct. 1995):128–57.

Simmons, R. G., M. Schimmel, and V. A. Butterworth. "The Self-Image of Unrelated Bone Marrow Donors." *Journal of Health and Social Behavior,* 34, no. 4 (Dec. 1993):285–301.

Respect

Livingston, J. S. "Pygmalion in Management." *Harvard Business Review,* Jan. 2003.

Rosenthal, R. *Pygmalion in the Classroom.* New York: Crown, 1992.

Tyler, K. "Extending the Olive Branch: Conflict Resolution Training Helps Employees and Managers Defuse Skirmishes." *HR Magazine,* Nov. 2002.

Williams, K. D. "Social Ostracism," in R. M. Kowalski. *Aversive Interpersonal Behaviors.* New York: Plenum, 1997.

Zeitlin, S., ed. *Because God Loves Stories.* New York: Touchstone 1997.

Flexibility

Robinson, L. "Interpersonal Relationship Quality in Young Adulthood: A Gender Analysis." *Adolescence,* Winter 2000.

Strayhorn, J. M. "Self-Control: Theory and Research." *Journal of the American Academy of Child and Adolescent Psychiatry,* Jan. 2002.

Memory
Demetrio, D. *Pedagogia della memoria.* Rome: Meltemi, 1998.
Marani, D. *Nuova grammatica finlandese.* Milan: Bompiani, 2002.

Loyalty
Buber, M. *The Legend of the Baal-Shem,* trans. M. Friedman. Princeton, NJ: Princeton University Press, 1995.
Ladd, G. W., B. J. Kochenderfer, and C. C. Coleman. "Friendship Quality as a Predictor of Young Children's Early School Adjustment." *Child Development,* 67, no. 3 (June 1996):1103–18.
Lepore, S. J. "Cynicism, Social Support, and Cardiovascular Reactivity." *Health Psychology,* 14, no. 3 (May 1995):210–16.
Stevens, N. "Friendship as a Key to Wellbeing: A Course for Women over 55 Years Old." *Tijdschrift voor gerontologie en geriatrie,* 28, no. 1 (Feb. 1997): 18–26.

Gratitude
Emmons, R. A., and C. A. Crumpler. "Gratitude as a Human Strength." *Journal of Social and Clinical Psychology,* 19, no. 1 (2000):56–69.
Emmons, R. A., and M. E. McCullough. "Counting Blessings Versus Burdens: An Experimental Investigation of Gratitude and Subjective Well-being in Daily Life." *Journal of Personality and Social Psychology,* 84, no. 2 (Feb. 2003):377–89.

Service
Caddy, E., and D. E. Platts. *Bringing More Love into Your Life: The Choice Is Yours.* Findhorn, Scotland: Findhorn, 1992.
Frizzel, B. "Self-Focused Attention in Depression and Its Relationship to Internal Self-Discrepancies and Rumination in Decision-Making." *Dissertation Abstracts International,* 53, no. 1-B9 (July 1992):562.

Gilbert, J. D. "Effects of Self-Focused Attention on Mood and Meta-Mood." *Dissertation Abstracts International,* 55, vol. 9-B (Mar. 1995):4157.

Huflejt-Lukasik, M. "Depression, Self-Focused Attention, and the Structure of Self-Standards." *Polish Psychological Bulletin,* 29, no. 1 (1998):33–45.

Ingram, R. E., and K. Wisnicki. "Situational Specificity of Self-Focused Attention in Disphoric States." *Cognitive Therapy and Research,* 23, no. 6 (Dec. 1999).

Jaffe, N., and S. Zeitlin. *The Cow of No Color.* New York: Henry Holt, 1998.

McFarland, C., and R. Buehler. "The Impact of Negative Affect on Autobiographical Memory: The Role of Self-Focused Attention to Moods." *Journal of Personality and Social Psychology,* 75, no. 6 (Dec. 1998):1424–40.

Miller, S. *Men and Friendship.* New York: Jeremy P. Tarcher, 1991.

Sakamoto, S. "The Relationship Between Rigidity of Self-Focused Attention and Depression." *Japanese Journal of Educational Psychology,* 41, no. 4 (Dec. 1993):407–13.

Schneider, B., and D. E. Bowen. "Understanding Customer Delight and Outrage." *Sloan Management Review,* Fall 1999.

Sullivan, G. B., and M. J. Sullivan. "Promoting Wellness in Cardiac Rehabilitation: Exploring the Role of Altruism." *Journal of Cardiovascular Nursing,* 11, no. 3 (Apr. 1997):43–52.

Thoits, P. A., and L. N. Hewitt. "Volunteer Work and Well-being." *Journal of Health and Social Behavior,* 42, no. 2 (June 2001):115–31.

Trout, S. *Born to Serve.* Alexandria, VA: Three Roses, 1997.

Joy

Brown, L. "Laughter: The Best Medicine." *Canadian Journal of Medical Radiation Technology,* 22, no. 3 (Aug. 1991):127–29.

Cohn, J. F., and E. Z. Tronick. "Three-Month-Old Infants' Reaction to Simulated Maternal Depression." *Child Development,* 54, no. 1 (Feb. 1983): 185–93.

Hassed, C. "How Humour Keeps You Well." *Australian Family Physician,* 30, no. 1 (Jan. 2001):25–28.

Peterson, C., and M. E. Seligman. "Character Strengths Before and After September 11." *Psychological Science,* 14, no. 4 (July 2003):381–84.

Ryan, R. M. "On Happiness and Human Potentials: A Review of Research on Hedonic and Eudaimonic Well-Being." *Annual Review of Psychology,* 2001.

Seligman, M. *Learned Optimism.* New York: Knopf, 1991.

Conclusion

"A Dalai Lama Treasury," *Shambhala Sun,* Sept. 2003:62.

Random Acts of Kindness. York Beach, ME: Conari, 1993.

ACKNOWLEDGMENTS

First of all, thanks to my wife for reading the Italian text and translating it into English. If you hadn't helped me, dear Vivien, this book would have been wordier and more sugary. Or maybe it would not have been at all. Thank you for being there—in my book and in my life.

Next I thank my agent, Linda Michaels: Dear Linda, you have been a wonderful help, before, during, and after the writing of this book, with your encouragement, inspiration, and concrete action. Let's continue like this!

Thanks to Laura Huxley: Dear Laura, from you I learned a lot about kindness and the art of living.

Thanks also to Andrea Bocconi: Dear Andrea, thank you for taking the trouble to read the manuscript and talk about it with me—the favor of a true friend.

Thank you, Teresa Cavanaugh, Marcella Meharg, and Ashley Shelby, for the advice you have given me.

And thank you to my children, relatives, friends, collaborators, teachers, students, and all those who have inspired me with their ideas and their kindness.

ABOUT THE AUTHOR

Piero Ferrucci was born in Turin, Italy, in 1946. After graduating with a degree in philosophy, he studied in Florence with Roberto Assagioli, the founder of psychosynthesis. Ferrucci edited Aldous Huxley's unpublished lectures, as the book *The Human Situation* (Harper, 1976), and is the author of *What We May Be* (Tarcher, 1982), *Inevitable Grace* (Tarcher, 1989), *Introduzione alla Psicosintesi* (Edizioni Mediterranee, 1993), and *What Our Children Teach Us* (Warner, 1997); with Laura Huxley, he has written *The Child of Your Dreams* (Inner Traditions International, 1987). His books have been published all over the world.

Ferrucci is a psychotherapist who has been practicing for thirty years in Florence. He lives with his wife and two sons in the Tuscan countryside.